GEORGE WASHINGTON

and the Birth of Our Nation

MILTON MELTZER

George Washington

AND THE BIRTH OF OUR NATION

Franklin Watts   New York   London   Toronto   Sydney
1986

Library of Congress Cataloging-in-Publication Data

Meltzer, Milton, 1915–
George Washington and the birth of our nation.

Bibliography: p.
Includes index.
Summary: A Biography of our first President, from
his growing-up years in Virginia to his death at
Mount Vernon.
1. Washington, George, 1732–1799—Juvenile
literature.   2. Presidents—United States
—Biography—Juvenile literature.   3. United
States—History—Revolution, 1775–1783
—Juvenile literature.   4. United States—
Politics and government—1783–1809—Juvenile
literature.   [1. Washington, George, 1732–
1799.   2. Presidents]   I. Title.
E312.66.M45   1986   973.4'1'0924   [B]   86-9222
ISBN 0-531-10253-X

For Anne, Gene,
Michael, and
Matthew Grandinetti

Maps by Vantage Art, Inc.

Photographs courtesy of:
New York Public Library Picture Collection:
pp. 19, 22, 24, 27, 35, 37, 56, 59, 69, 72,
73, 77, 101, 119, 122, 140, 174; The Mount
Vernon Ladies' Association: pp. 30, 171;
Bettman Archive: pp. 46, 51, 82, 88, 112,
136, 149, 161; Washington/Custis/Lee
Collection, Washington and Lee University,
Virginia: p. 64; The Granger Collection:
pp. 85, 166; Library of Congress: pp. 89,
146; Yale University Art Gallery: pp. 90, 94;
The Metropolitan Museum of Art, Bequest
of William H. Huntington, 1885: p. 109;
National Archives: p. 131; The New York
Historical Society, New York City: p. 142.

CONTENTS

GEORGE WASHINGTON

and the Birth of Our Nation

INTRODUCTION

George Washington. That monument? Those statues? That face on the dollar bill? That head carved on Mount Rushmore? The bridge? The capital? The state, the counties, the towns and villages, the mountains, the lakes, the public squares, the colleges all called by his name?

No, the *man*. The real man, the man who lived so long ago it's hard to remember he was human.

But he was. He wasn't GEORGE WASHINGTON when he was born. He was an infant, given a name like any other name that means nothing to anyone but the family. And then he grew up. And near the end of a life rich in great experiences was turned into a monument after whom Americans would name a thousand sons and things and places.

The human being becomes lost when that happens. The truth lies buried beneath the legends and the falsehoods. What the man was really like this book tries to suggest. He was just as individual as you or I. Different from others in some ways, yet the same in many other ways. Just as hard to understand, yet just as easy to like or to love when you get to know him with all his strengths and failings, his humor and anger, his doubts and certainties.

CHAPTER ONE

Growing Up in Virginia

George—let's call him that, at least until he reaches manhood—lived in an America vastly different from ours. When he was born, more than 250 years ago, America was part of the British empire. The thirteen American colonies stretched down the Atlantic seacoast from Maine to Georgia. The pioneers had not yet scaled the Appalachians to settle the interior. Still, the land they built their homes on was enormous. Its forests were thick, its fields fertile, its shores and rivers teemed with fish.

British America's resources were infinite, but as yet scarcely touched. The population was tiny—only 600,000 souls. (About the same number who now live in Boston, Massachusetts.) Most of the people lived on the countryside. They were hardworking farmers, fishermen, woodsmen, who made a modest living or were downright poor. The vast majority of immigrants came from European farms they had worked for landlords. In America they were much more likely to own their land. Those who could not pay the ship passage often came as indentured servants. That is, in exchange for the fare, they contracted to give a certain number of years of labor. Thousands more came unwillingly—as slaves from Africa. Others were convicts sentenced to terms of labor in the colonies, or kidnapped children or vagabonds. Many served out their terms, then farmed or practiced a trade on their own.

The colonists provided lumber, rice, indigo, tobacco, furs, and ship supplies for use or sale in Great Britain. In return, they got all kinds of manufactured goods—clothing, glass, clocks, books, kettles, carpenter's tools. In their scattered towns the colonists carried on trade and manufactured some goods. There were only a handful of such centers in George's youth, and they were nothing like the cities of today. They had a few hundred or a few thousand inhabitants at most. All of them sat on the seacoast or at the mouth of navigable rivers. Less than 5 percent of the Americans lived in such places.

Infant industries grew up to exploit the high quality of America's raw materials. From the great forest, workers made many timber products especially for shipbuilding. From the plentiful mineral deposits, an iron industry developed that became one of the largest in the world. Milling products and New England rum became flourishing industries too. On the farms, people made their own necessities—clothing, shoes, furniture, kitchen utensils, beer.

The young America George was born into was already divided into social classes. There were the rich, the poor, and the enslaved, and in between the middle class. Most Americans mistakenly believe George was born an aristocrat and enjoyed the benefits of wealth and the best education. Not so. George entered the world on February 22, 1732, at Bridges' Creek, near the Potomac in Virginia. His great-grandfather was a poor English adventurer who had emigrated to Virginia. John Washington left a villainous reputation. His business practices were unsavory and he was implicated in the murder of five Indian ambassadors.

But as Virginia prospered, so did the Washingtons, though they never achieved great wealth or position. They had friends among the aristocrats, and George himself would marry into that class. George's father, Augustine, was a restless man, unsure of himself, given to making deals that lost money and often landed him in the law courts. He married twice. Two sons survived the first marriage, and from the second, five children, of whom George was the oldest.

Soon after George's birth the family moved forty miles upriver to a farm that would later become famous as Mount Vernon. When he was six they moved again, thirty miles southeast, to a farm near the Rappahannock River across from Fredericksburg, the first town George had ever seen. An inventory of family possessions made when George was eleven shows what, besides land, they owned: sixteen pairs of sheets and seventeen pillowcases, thirteen beds and a couch, desks, chests, chairs, a fireplace set, tablecloths, napkins, a looking glass, one silver-plated soup spoon, eighteen small spoons, seven teaspoons, a watch, a sword, and eleven China plates. George's father listed twenty slaves, seven of them able-bodied, eight of moderate value, and five unable to work because they were too young or too old.

George's mother, Mary Ball Washington, was orphaned when very young. Left a tidy estate and with no parents to control her, she became very self-centered. At twenty-three she had married Augustine. She seems to have given George, her first-born, little reason to love her. He would always treat her politely, although she criticized everything he did, complained constantly that he neglected her, and was forever asking for money.

Soon after the family settled in at Ferry Farm, as they called the new place, the education of George began. Seven was the usual age for teaching children to read and write and to handle numbers. Virginia, like most of the colonies, had no public schools. Most children studied at home. If they mastered their ABCs, they used them chiefly to read the Bible and religious tracts. The year George was born, Benjamin Franklin published his *Poor Richard's Almanac*, a best-seller that offered weather forecasts, recipes, and children's primers as well as witty advice on how to get rich quick.

George's exercise books show he had a large, clear hand. His was a practical education. He learned arithmetic to help him keep accounts and geometry to prepare him for surveying. He studied geography and a bit of astronomy. He copied out poems and over 100 maxims from the *Rules of Civility and Decent Behavior in Company and Conversation*. Among them were such gems as "Cleanse not your teeth with the tablecloth," "Kill no vermin in the sight of others," and "Keep to the fashion of your equals." Later he coined maxims of his own and handed them out liberally in letters to young people.

George liked to read books that would teach him something useful or give him pleasure. He had an eye for symmetry. His calligraphy and mathematical diagrams are careful and artistic. His father had sent George's two

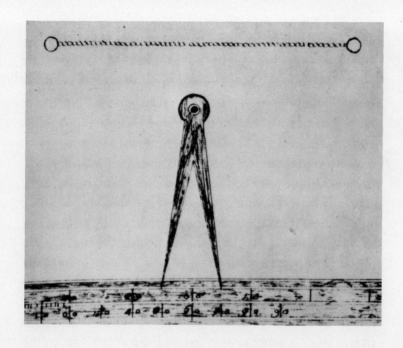

George taught himself the surveyor's skills in his early teens. This chain, compass, and scale were drawn by him when he was fourteen.

half-brothers to England for schooling, but the youngest son never went abroad. His formal education stopped in his early teens. Whatever he learned thereafter came from worldly experience, conversation, or reading. He regretted not having a better education, which may explain why he spoke little in public and did not write his own account of his Revolutionary and Presidential years. He was one of the few presidents whose formal schooling did not go beyond the level of elementary school. But he never stopped learning from living.

His boyhood embraced more than tutors and copy-books. George began riding horseback when a little boy. He became a splendid rider, admired for his skill and grace. His remarkable physical strength was developed in the rough sports typical of boyhood. The river that flowed in front of the house offered fishing and boating and swimming. He often crossed the Rappahannock to explore Fredericksburg, its wharfs and quarries, the courthouse and the stone jail, the tobacco warehouses and the English ships docking to unload their cargoes.

When George was about eight the brother he adored—Lawrence, fourteen years older—joined a colonial regiment that sailed off to help Britain fight Spain in the Caribbean. George admired Lawrence in his splendid captain's uniform and loved to hear of the battles on land and sea. He never forgot his brother's bitter stories of the British general who scorned the American colonials and neglected them while they died of disease.

Just after Lawrence's return from war, George's father died. He left 10,000 acres in several tracts and 49 slaves. The estate was split several ways. George's share was Ferry Farm, an unproductive property, about 2,000 acres on another tract that was just as poor, and 10 slaves. Because he was only eleven, his mother was given control of the estate until George would reach twenty-one. That proved a disaster. Mary Washington had no business sense but refused to admit it. She failed to let go of George's inheritance until he was almost forty, though her husband had provided for her in his will.

Although most widows remarried, Mary Washington did not. With his two half-brothers managing their own estates, George at eleven became the substitute father of his siblings—a sister and three brothers. His mother was a powerful woman, frightening to her children. Unhappy under her vigilant eye, George escaped home as often as he could, visiting his half-brothers and even distant cousins. He learned early from his mother how one's own actions affect the feelings of others. It was a lesson in decent human behavior that stood him well in his future career.

It was Lawrence who opened a window on how the rich live. Now the owner of the Potomac estate he had renamed Mount Vernon, Lawrence married Anne Fairfax, daughter of one of Virginia's great aristocratic families. The Fairfaxes lived on a nearby estate called Belvoir. Their handsome brick mansion gave young George a taste of elegance and grandeur. The master of Belvoir was William Fairfax, a distant relative of Lord Fairfax, who had been given five million acres of Virginia under a royal grant. As the Fairfax man in the colony, William had great power. It was influence he had done nothing to earn. Simply by being born into the right family, he enjoyed favors that lifted him to the seat of power.

William's own son was a dull weakling ignored by his father. Though seven years older than George, the young heir treated George as a close friend while his father welcomed the far more vital George as a son. George observed how important influence was if you wanted to move up in the world. When George was fourteen, the Fairfaxes offered to get him an appointment in the Royal Navy. The boy hesitated, but then packed his bags to join the fleet. Suddenly his mother took back her approval and insisted he stay home. George was glad; he had no desire for a life at sea. (What would have happened to American history had his talents moved him high in His Majesty's Navy?)

Fox hunting with his aristocratic neighbors, the Fairfaxes, was a sport Washington much enjoyed.

There was more excitement when Lord Fairfax himself arrived from England with trunks full of the latest fashion in clothes and with his own pack of hunting hounds. The great rooms at Belvoir were crowded with relatives and friends paying court in the hope of obtaining money or position or a generous slice of his lordship's lands. These hangers-on showed no interest in doing anything productive with their lives. The way they played the game of influence fascinated George and surely must have tempted him. But suddenly the Fairfaxes turned him in the opposite direction from the aristocrat's soft life. They sent him over the Blue Ridge Mountains into the frontier. He was to work with a surveying party to lay out his lordship's lands in the Shenandoah Valley in farm-size lots.

CHAPTER TWO

The Young Surveyor

George had just turned sixteen when he headed west on his first trip to the frontier. In the last few years he had grown rapidly. He was more than six feet tall (a great height in those days), slender but strong, with long arms and legs, and large hands and feet. His eyes were a light greenish blue and his hair hazel brown. He spoke slowly, thinking first about what he had to say.

A year before the Fairfax mission he had already carried out his first professional survey. He had learned how by studying a few books on the surveyor's art and trying out the tools his father left him. He began to earn small fees as assistant to surveyors in the neighborhood. The area George grew up in had a measureless abundance of cheap land that called for surveying. The average estate was 700 acres; many were thousands more. The Virginia colony had been started as a money-making venture by a company of English investors. When their projects failed, the King stepped in and made Virginia the first royal colony.

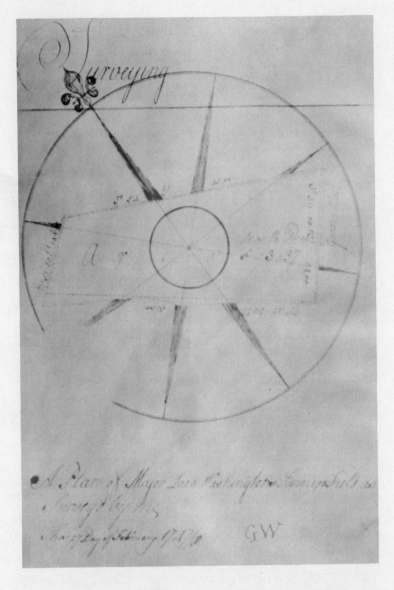

The plan of a relative's turnip field "as Survey'd by me"
—drawn in George's school copybook in 1747 and signed "GW"

Profits blossomed when the native tobacco plant was brought to England and smoking became the rage in all the courts of Europe. The fashion turned tobacco into the number one crop in Virginia. Raising it required a big supply of field labor; there never were enough hands in the early years. And tobacco soon exhausted the soil. The first problem was solved by the importation of slaves from Africa. The second required more and more fresh land each year. That led to the grabbing up of any land a planter could get away with, and to speculation in the buying and selling of land. By George's time Virginia listed over 6,000 plantations, big and small. The big ones kept getting bigger. The small ones were pushed farther inland where the white farmers worked the land by their own labor.

The Tidewater estates, stretching back some seventy-five miles from the ocean, depended on the labor of slaves. By now their number was greater than the colony's white population. The slaves were the bottom class in Virginia. Above them were the indentured servants, and then the class made up of farmers, mechanics, hunters, fishermen. Many of these poor folk lived in miserable squalor in crude huts. Their chance of betterment was almost zero. In the middle class were small tobacco farmers and landowners, shopkeepers, and the owners of small fishing boats. Some of them could hope to improve their lot.

George, as we've seen, was not born into a ruling family. But his father, grandfather, and great-grandfather had all become justices of the peace—a position of authority and prestige. His father had also been a sheriff and churchwarden, which added to his standing. His half-brother Lawrence was now a burgess, or member of the legislature, as well as a trustee of the town of Alexandria. Lawrence's marriage into the powerful Fairfax family was a great asset to George. It gave him close ties to a ruling family and led to his present commission on Virginia's frontier.

Settlers were beginning to push across the Alleghenies to the great central plain of North America. George was already familiar with back country; it lay only a day's ride west from both Ferry Farm and Mount Vernon. On this, his first real adventure, he learned what backwoods living was like. In his journal he wrote:

> We got our supper and was lighted into a room and I, not being as good a woodsman as the rest of my company, stripped myself very orderly and went in to the bed, as they called it, when to my surprise, I found it to be nothing but a little straw matted together, without sheets or anything else, but only one threadbare blanket, with double its weight of vermin, such as lice, fleas, etc., and I was glad to get up, as soon as the light was carried from us. I put on my clothes, and lay as my companions (on the floor).

The next day the group found a more civilized inn, with "wine and rum punch in plenty, and a good feather bed with clean sheets." As he entered the Shenandoah Valley he was struck with the beauty of the sugar maples and the richness of the land. The roads were terrible, and rainy nights a misery. They swam their horses across a river swollen with melted snow from the mountains. One night the straw they lay on caught fire; luckily a man woke in time to give the alarm.

They ran into a party of thirty Indians returning from war with a trophy of one scalp. George's group shared some liquor with them, which set the Indians to

At sixteen, George went on his first surveying expedition, in the Shenandoah Valley.

demonstrate a war dance. For music one Indian drummed on a pot half-full of water with a deerskin stretched tight over it, while another shook a gourd with some shot rattling in it. George showed little interest in Indian ways; it would be a long time before interest in their culture would develop.

The next day the surveyors came upon German settlers who had settled illegally on Lord Fairfax's empty land. Would the farms they had created out of their muscle and sweat be taken away? George's journal makes no mention of that. He only displays a snobbish disdain because they spoke no English, only "Dutch."

For thirty-three days in blustery March and April weather George practiced surveying, often in pelting rain. He began to feel like a pioneer. Once he paddled forty miles upriver through turbulent water. He shot wild turkeys, got lost for a day in the Blue Ridge Mountains, faced down a rattlesnake, cooked his meals over a spit of forked sticks. The flowering meadows, the lofty rock ledges, the starry skies, the sound of rushing water as he lay awake by a fire in the open, excited in him a love of the West he would never lose.

Home again, George had great stories to tell. Some had a practical edge: he had seen how speculators raced into the empty valleys, buying up land cheap and selling it dear to the next wave of settlers. His brother Lawrence decided to buy 1,300 acres in the Shenandoah George had just explored. If he had the money George would do the same. To get it he took on surveying jobs. But life was more than business ventures. He read some English history and amused himself at billiards. He played card games for decent stakes and under Lawrence's guidance learned to dance, to dress well, and to practice the manners of the first families of Virginia.

That winter George's friend young Fairfax married Sally Cary, a beautiful and charming eighteen-year-old neighbor. George's hours in her company would be the happiest he would ever know, as he confessed late in life. He fell in love with his friend's wife, and until his death thought of her often.

Life among the aristocrats he visited at Belvoir made George aware of how far he had to climb if he was ever to reach their position. He knew people judged their condition not by what it truly was but by comparison with others. Yes, he had enough to eat and decent clothes to wear and his mother's roof over his head. But Ferry Farm looked shabby next to Belvoir. And sometimes George could not ride to the dancing assemblies because he couldn't afford the feed for his horse.

When he was seventeen, the Fairfaxes gave him another assignment: making the surveys for the new town of Alexandria on the Potomac. Then he crossed the Blue Ridge again to do more surveys in the Shenandoah. To a friend he wrote: "I have not slept above three nights or four in a bed, but, after walking a good deal all the day lay down before the fire upon a little hay, straw, fodder, or bearskin—whichever is to be had—with man, wife, and children like a parcel of dogs or cats, and happy's he that gets the berth nearest the fire."

Happy too was George with his keen eye for the girls. Sally was out of bounds, of course, but there were other "agreeable young ladies," as he put it, in the Fairfax

Lawrence Washington, George's older
half brother, and his best friend

circle. From the bad poems he wrote in his teens it's plain he was in love with love. He enjoyed flirting at parties and dances but he did not have the easy charm to captivate the young women. Perhaps his extraordinary size and the quiet power people sensed in him put them off. Still, there is some evidence of at least three love affairs by the time he was twenty.

As George was moving into full manhood, a family disaster shattered his happiness. His brother Lawrence and his wife lost three children one after the other, and then Lawrence himself took sick with tuberculosis. Local medicine could do nothing; it was thought a tropical climate might help. George accompanied his brother on the long voyage to Barbados, only to watch helplessly as his beloved Lawrence coughed away his life. George himself was seized with pain and a burning fever that turned into the ugly eruption of smallpox. It left him with a pitted nose but he was lucky; it also left him immune to the disease that would be the greatest killer of the American Revolution.

The death of his brother and best friend was the deepest tragedy of George's life. Gone at thirty-four, Lawrence left huge debts and a troublesome will. He gave George a few lots and the remote hope of acquiring Mount Vernon, should he survive Lawrence's widow. Lawrence had been Adjutant General of Virginia, which meant he supervised the training of the colony's volunteer military company. George began to pull strings with influential friends to get that vacant post. At the age of twenty he was made Major Washington and told to train the militia of one of Virginia's four military districts. It seemed potential enemies had little to fear—George had absolutely none of the skills the job called for.

Still, it was quite an achievement for a man not yet twenty-one. And he was not only an adjutant, but the owner of 1,500 acres in the Shenandoah (bought with his own earnings) and the official surveyor of Culpepper County. George was learning all the arts of making his way in the world.

CHAPTER THREE

The Taste of Combat

George turned twenty-one at a time when England and France were contending for power in the world. Britain's colonies in America flanked the eastern seaboard up to the Alleghenies. The French holdings ran in a great arc up the St. Lawrence River through the Great Lakes, and down the Mississippi to New Orleans. The two empires had been warring off and on for about fifty years. If France solidified her claims to the Ohio valley it would block the American colonies from the west. But if Britain entrenched herself in the Ohio valley, it would break the French barrier and open the way to control of the Mississippi. At this moment there was an uneasy peace between the two powers, but it was only an armed truce. Each waited for the right moment to spring.

Virginia investors, among them Governor Dinwiddie, William Fairfax, and Lawrence Washington, had years before set up an Ohio Company to trade in furs and speculate in land in that huge territory. The Company had secured from the British Crown a grant of half a million acres. The trouble was, the King of France

—33

claimed that land too. To secure its rights the Company decided to built a fort where the Monongahela and Allegheny rivers came together. It would be both a trading center and a strong defense point. Then came word that the French had already begun building a chain of forts running south from Lake Erie to the Ohio.

The Governor sent the alarming news to London. Back came orders from George II to send a mission into the wilderness to see what the French were up to. Build a fort there, the king said; if the French refuse to leave peaceably, then "drive them out by force of arms." The message pleased the Ohio investors, for they would profit by it. But the Governor knew that wilderness wars with the French were not popular. So without consulting his legislature, he picked George Washington to carry the royal word to the French in the wilderness.

It was late October of 1753 when George and his six men set out for the Ohio country. If he could successfully carry out his combined military and diplomatic mission, his reputation would be made. Despite his youth, he had been chosen because he was an insider who would keep secrets, he knew the frontier, and he was a hardworking and responsible man. He looked like a leader too, standing six feet, three-and-a-half inches tall, and weighing nearly two hundred pounds.

With him was a tough frontiersman, Christopher Gist; Van Daam, a Dutchman who could serve as interpreter with the French; and four servants. George's orders were to contact friendly Indians to find out where the French forces were, then to spy out their strength and determine their intentions. He had an official letter to

George on his mission to the frontier region of
the Ohio Valley. At twenty-one, he was picked
by the Governor of Virginia to head the military
and diplomatic expedition into the wilderness.

present which politely demanded that the French with-draw from English territory.

George's party pushed up the steep divide between the Shenandoah and Ohio valleys, slowed by heavy rains and early winter snows. It took a week to go seventy-five miles. Reaching the Forks of the Ohio, George studied the terrain and decided to relocate the planned fort so that it would give command over the two rivers. His party called on a chief of the Delaware Indians and then stopped at an Iroquois town to seek their help. Their leader told George that they had nothing against trading with either the French or the British, but would not submit to either power's building houses upon their land and taking it by force. The land belonged to neither the French nor the British, he said, "but the Great Being above."

Not asked what his mission was, George kept silent. Had he told the Indians they would again have just cause for anger. The British had all too often assumed the Indians could be manipulated to suit imperial interests. The Indians knew from long experience that the aim of the whites was rather to steal their land than to trade with them.

Early in December the party met some French officers in the wilderness, and with them advanced another sixty miles through swamp and snows to Fort LeBoeuf on French Creek. George was allowed to wander at will about the fort and take notes. He saw a garrison of some 100 men plus officers, and a fleet of about 300 canoes on the river. But the French commandant made plain that his master, King Louis XV, had no intention of giving up his rights to the lands on the Ohio River.

With the frontiersman Christopher Gist, George poles a raft across the icy Allegheny River, on the way back to Williamsburg.

George left the French in a desperate hurry to reach the Governor with the bad news. With winter choking the trails and rivers with ice and snow the way back was hard and dangerous. An Indian shot at George almost point-blank but luckily missed. They caught him and Gist wanted to kill him. But George let him go free, accepting the Indian's plea that it was an accident. They traveled day and night, built a raft to cross the half-frozen Allegheny, and almost lost George again when the wild water tossed him overboard and he nearly drowned.

Eleven weeks after his mission began, George was back in Williamsburg with his grim news. The Governor gave him twenty-four hours to write a detailed report that could be printed up for the Virginia Assembly and forwarded to London. The tone of the direct and honest account is amazingly self-confident for so young a man. There is nothing I couldn't handle, he seems to be saying cockily. The Assembly voted him £50 in approval; George thought it mighty small pay for a winter journey "few or none would have undertaken." A gripe, but George knew his star was rising. In London and Paris weren't kings and generals studying his report?

The Governor ordered a small military expedition to hold the Ohio country, and raising him to Lieutenant Colonel, chose George as second in command. It didn't upset George. To be Number One, he wrote a friend, "would be a charge too great for my youth and inexperience." His superior was an aging math teacher with even less military experience. Indians reported that a big French force was coming downriver to the Forks where the Virginians were building their fort. Dinwiddie ordered George to recruit his troops rapidly and move at once to the Ohio. If the French interfered with the fort or settlement, he was to restrain them. If they refused to depart, he was to attack them.

The problems George had to solve were enormous. Where would he get soldiers quickly? How would he find the money to pay and clothe them? Where would food and military supplies come from? If he had been more experienced he would have felt despair. But he was too innocent to realize what lay ahead.

Few men wanted to volunteer for a frontier war. Farmers refused to rent their horses and wagons to carry supplies and, when ordered to, hid them. It took a month to gather 150 men and 8 subordinate officers, some rickety wagons, old nags, and a few cannon. The soldiers lacked shoes, stockings, shirts, and tents to shelter them in a cold and wet season.

There was no road across the Alleghenies. The men had to chop their way through the forest. Three weeks out, they met a small band of Virginians— garrison troops who had fled the unfinished fort at the Forks when a thousand French troops had canoed in and invited them to leave or be wiped out. They refused to join George's men and he sent them back to Virginia under guard.

Eager for action, George decided to move on to the Monongahela, where the Ohio Company had built a warehouse. This would place them only forty miles from where the French were building a stronghold they called Fort Duquesne.

The advance over the steep rise of the Alleghenies was rough and slow. It took fifteen days for the wagon train to make twenty miles. But they opened the Ohio valley for the first time to wheeled vehicles. Held up by a river in flood, George complained in a letter to the Governor that the American officers were getting lower pay than the British regulars serving in the colonies. Why should our lives be worth less than theirs? If he was concerned about their pride, he was also concerned about their pockets. Were it not for the close danger they faced, his officers would resign. As for himself, he would refuse any pay and serve as a volunteer.

Again they marched ahead, to learn from Indian scouts that some thirty or so French troops were hiding nearby. Early the next morning, George attacked. His men routed the French in a brief skirmish. Ten of the French were killed, including their commander; twenty-two were taken prisoner. The French angrily accused him of murdering an ambassador. They meant their commander, who carried diplomatic instructions to find the English and peaceably warn them off land the French owned. To the inexperienced young Colonel this charge didn't amount to much. He thought the "diplomatic immunity" was merely a screen for the intention to attack. To him there was a basic conflict between the two powers. He had adopted a surprise tactic and weren't the results satisfactory?

So small an encounter gave the signal that set Europe and America ablaze. George had shed the first blood in the Seven Years' War (called the French and Indian War in America). It would cost the lives of more than a million soldiers and civilians.

The victory raised George's confidence in himself. And it gave him an unwarranted contempt for the French. The Governor praised him and promoted him to Colonel of the Virginia Regiment. It worried George that he still had no experienced officer to command him. But at least reinforcements reached him—another 200 troops and 3 officers.

An Indian reported that the French at the Forks were sending 800 soldiers and 400 Indian allies to attack George's smaller force. He decided to make his stand at a place called Fort Necessity. In his inexperience he made the stockade so small it could not contain his troops. In front he placed a ditch and an earthen parapet. He ignored the fact that a wooded height overlooked the fort.

A battle began early on July 3, 1754. The French and Indians took cover on the heights and angled their fire into the fort. It was a horror that dragged on for hours. Only the inaccuracy of the firearms of that time saved George's men from being wiped out. With the afternoon came a heavy rain that turned the fort into a bloody catchbasin. The rain ruined the ammunition and the stores of gunpowder. Still, George didn't think of surrendering. His surviving troops kept firing, perhaps because they had broken into the rum kegs to keep up their spirits.

When darkness fell the French offered to parley. In the ceasefire George counted a third of his men dead or wounded. There was almost no food or ammunition left. Hopeless, he had to give in. The French allowed him to march out under arms and take his beaten men back to Virginia.

More than once on this mission George had been given good advice by friendly Indians. But he was the victim of both ignorance and prejudice, and did not listen. Like almost all whites, he saw the Native Americans through the glass of his own culture. The image was badly distorted. From their first arrival in the New World, whites had believed the red people they found here were hardly human. Who could understand these "savages," or bother to try?

George did confess on his mission that "for want of a better acquaintance with their customs, I am often at a loss how to behave." His exposure of his troops to massacre by a vastly superior enemy seemed madness to his Indian allies. They did not consider any of their people expendable. Their approach to combat was to injure the enemy with the least loss to themselves. That was why their favorite tactic was ambush. They had fore-seen George's defeat at Fort Necessity; it made no sense to them.

The lesson the Indians drew from these battles was that the conflict between the two European powers was not their fight. They would ally themselves with whatever side looked to be the winner. With George's defeat at Fort Necessity, they decided to cast their lot with the French.

At home in Virginia, George's many mistakes were overlooked. He was hailed as a hero for his brave lead-ership against superior odds. Now that Britain was at war with France, he expected the Crown to make his Virginia Regiment part of the regular British Army. And that of course would mean his commission as a colonel in that army. But the British command laughed at the idea. To them, George and his troops were only the latest example of clumsy colonials. George saw his regiment broken up and was told no colonial would be given a commission higher than captain.

In his pride he would not accept being reduced to captain. He felt poorly rewarded for what he had done. Yes, he liked the taste of combat, and still yearned for the military life. But it was humiliating to be treated this way. He resigned from service.

CHAPTER FOUR

A *Struggle for Empire*

*L*ate in 1754 George decided it was time to leave Ferry Farm (and his mother) and establish his own home. His sister-in-law, Lawrence's widow, had remarried and moved out of Mount Vernon. He leased the estate from her—house, plantation and 18 slaves—for 15,000 pounds of tobacco per year. It would be his home until his death. All he needed to round out his domestic life was to find a wife.

But that search would have to wait. The British had decided to capture Fort Duquesne from the French and sent two regular regiments to make sure the colonial forces would succeed this time. In March 1755 British troops under command of Major General Edward Braddock sailed up the Potomac past Mount Vernon and landed at Alexandria. George watched his first review of professional soldiers and marvelled at the precision of their maneuvers on the parade ground.

George's friends let Braddock know that the young veteran would like to serve with him. Braddock had learned that no one knew more about the wilderness his troops would have to march through than this colonial. He invited George to an interview. As George was leaving for the appointment his mother dashed up to Mount Vernon. She had heard of his desire to serve king and country but insisted that if he went he would be neglecting his duty to her. Finally she walked out, furious with his stubborn independence. He met Braddock, who was much taken with the colonial soldier. When the general could not offer him a suitable rank, George agreed to serve on his staff without rank or pay. He would be a volunteer aide.

As usual, there was great delay in securing the supplies, horses, and wagons Braddock needed. The force of some 2,000 men finally set out to march the 150 miles to Fort Duquesne. Braddock was a stubby, elderly man with over forty years of service but little combat action behind him. George found him to be a rudely blunt officer who knew nothing about wilderness warfare. He meant to fight the enemy the way they did in Europe—armies meeting armies on the fields of battle. As so often happens, he was trained for the last war, fought in another place, not this war in this place.

George, the expert on frontier conditions, tried to educate the general and his staff on the need to plan their attack for the way the Canadian French and the Indians would fight. But they were too fixed in their old ways. Braddock offended the few Indians still willing to help the British by his arrogant indifference to what they had to say. The Indians soon disappeared.

Acting as though they were in Europe, the British army began to build a fine road through the mountains. But it advanced the troops only two miles a day. George saw it would delay them so much that the French would have time to bring reinforcements up to Fort Duquesne. He urged Braddock to move ahead rapidly by pack horse instead of on wheels. That's not my way, the general said. Then George came down with violent fever and pain (probably dysentery) and had to stay behind to recover. Growing impatient at the slowness of their advance, Braddock now accepted George's plan to move 1,200 troops rapidly ahead, with pack horses to carry supplies. The rest of the army would follow more slowly with the heavy artillery.

Still quite ill, George feared missing battle and insisted on moving up in a wagon. He found Braddock near the Monongahela, only twelve miles from Fort Duquesne. The army's campfires lit up the Ohio woods. The next day, July 9, he got up at dawn, eager to be part of a maneuver everyone believed would end in the taking of the fort. He had to tie pillows to his saddle to be able to ride. He joined Braddock and his aides crossing the Monongahela on the way to the French fort. As they rode ahead a shot echoed through the woods, followed by Indian shrieks and howls and then the sound of heavy firing. The advance guard was under attack.

Braddock, with George beside him, led the main column forward. Suddenly the twelve-foot road between the trees was filled with red-coated soldiers racing back toward them in panicky flight. George and the other officers shouted commands to halt, "with as much success," he said later, "as if we had attempted to have stopped the wild bears of the mountains." The runaways slammed into the advancing troops, wrecking all order. At the same moment rifle fire flashed from the woods on

*Against the advice of his young aide, Washington,
General Braddock marches his troops in close formation
toward Fort Duquesne. The long column of red-coats
was slaughtered by the French and their Indian allies.*

both sides as the Indians, hidden behind the trees, cut
down the terrified troops. The road piled high with bloody
bodies. The officers on horseback made easy targets. Those
still in the saddle wheeled in circles, hitting the men
with the flats of their swords as they tried to stop the
rout. George's horse went down under him. He jumped
free and leaped on a riderless horse dashing past. He felt

a terrible rage as the demoralized soldiers paid no attention to commands. The British regulars were not trained to fight out of formation, on their own. They huddled in the road and firing blindly ahead, shot into the backs of their own men. The officers tried madly to regroup the men into parade-ground formations.

When George begged Braddock to let him lead the colonial soldiers into the woods to fight the enemy in their own way, the general angrily refused. Bullets ripped through George's coat. Braddock toppled over, a bullet piercing a lung. George lost his second horse from under him and then a bullet tore off his hat. But "the miraculous care of Providence protected me beyond all human expectation," as he wrote later. So many officers had been killed or wounded that George was the only one left to carry out the wounded Braddock's orders. When Braddock slipped into a coma George placed him in a covered cart and led the retreat across the river of those men still able to move. They abandoned almost 900 men dead or wounded on the field of slaughter, where their scalps were harvested by the triumphant Indians.

Coming out of the coma, Braddock refused to give over command. He ordered George to ride back forty miles through the night to bring up reinforcements. Sick, exhausted by twelve hours in the saddle, shaken by the terrible sight of the dead and the dying, the groans and pitiful cries of the wounded for help, George felt unable to carry out the command. But somehow he summoned up his astounding young strength and started through the dark woods. At times unable to see the road in the blackness, he had to dismount and crawl on hands and knees to feel his way. He reached his goal, but news of the massacre had got there ahead of him. The soldiers and even the officers were too terrified to follow orders.

Braddock died and George buried him deep beneath the road they had cut. The remnants of the British army fled to Philadelphia. George rode slowly and painfully back to Mount Vernon. Duquesne was still in the hands of the French.

How had this disaster happened? The British force had seemed invincible. Who could have expected this outcome? "The uncertainty of human things!" George wrote.

Despite Braddock's defeat, George's own reputation prospered throughout the colonies. Benjamin Franklin praised him, and a preacher wondered if God had not preserved George Washington because he was destined for some great service to his country. Even the British regular officers he had served with said he had shown "the greatest courage and resolution."

The war between the English and French moved northward, into the wilderness that separated Canada and New York. George paid little attention to battles fought outside his own colony. He knew Virginia's long frontier now lay wide open to hit-and-run Indian raids. His task for the next two years would be to defend the distant settlers. Made Colonel of the Virginia Regiment, he was given full command of all the forces. Pick your own officers and procure your own supplies, he was told. So now, at twenty-three, he had the whole burden of defense on his shoulders.

It was a task that would have frightened anyone else. How could a few hundred men protect a 350-mile border? The colony's draft laws went easy on the rich and hard on the poor. The rich could avoid the draft by paying cash or providing a paid substitute. The poor were stuck; they could not afford the options of the rich and often were so badly off they took cash to serve in place of the rich. No wonder one out of four men deserted. It took all the authority and persuasion and threats George could muster to hold even a small force together. Once in desperation he hanged two deserters from a high gallows in front of the troops. When even that ghastly spectacle failed to stop the runaways, pity drove him to pardon a new batch of deserters sentenced to death. The strain was so great he thought of resigning. Yet he did not; he felt too responsible for his fellow frontiersmen to let them down.

George also had to deal with conscientious objectors, men who would take no part in war because they opposed the use of violence. When seven young Quakers resisted the draft they were arrested and sentenced to do work at a fort under George's command. They refused to do anything that would aid the military. George threatened them each with 500 lashes. They stuck to their principles and, impressed by their faith in their beliefs, he relented. He kept them under house arrest until their year's service was up, then let them go.

Late in 1757 George again came down with dysentery and was bled three times by an army doctor—a common but useless medical treatment of those days. Gravely sick, he was forced to leave his command and go home to Mount Vernon. He feared he would soon die—die young, as his father and brother had done before him. In the spring he felt well enough to go back into action. Indian raids had dropped over the winter; now they revived again. George begged the authorities to strengthen the regular army and give up on temporary troops who only consumed his supplies and then fled at rumors of Indian raids. His appeal did nothing but bring criticism upon himself. That he managed to keep his small force in the field against such odds was a tribute to his qualities as a leader. His officers were passionately devoted to him. He chose them for their ability, not their connections, and he promoted them solely on merit. They knew he stood for justice.

The British again decided to advance on Fort Duquesne. Instead of taking the old route across the mountains that George knew so well, an army began to cut a new road westward from Pennsylvania. George urged in vain that his road was better and faster. The army was still plodding toward the Ohio Forks when the French suddenly burned down Fort Duquesne and gave up the Ohio valley.

It was a strange and bloodless anti-climax. Now, after five years of soldiering, George felt he could resign. Peace had returned to the Virginia frontier. This was the time to end his military career.

The conflict in North America went on. To London it seemed a mere sideshow to the great war raging between the contending empires of Europe. When the British took the French base at Quebec, Canada fell. And with it, France fell. The Treaty of Paris in 1763 ended the war. The winner took over all French possessions in Canada and east of the Mississippi. The almost unknown country beyond the great river stayed in the hands of Spain. With the barrier down, English settlers and speculators could turn west. Expansion there was safe now.

Washington raises the British flag at Fort Duquesne when the French abandoned it. It marked the return of peace to the Virginia frontier.

The peace treaty promised to create an American empire. But word came from London that the Americans were not to move into this new land. The territory was to be held for use by the mother country at some future

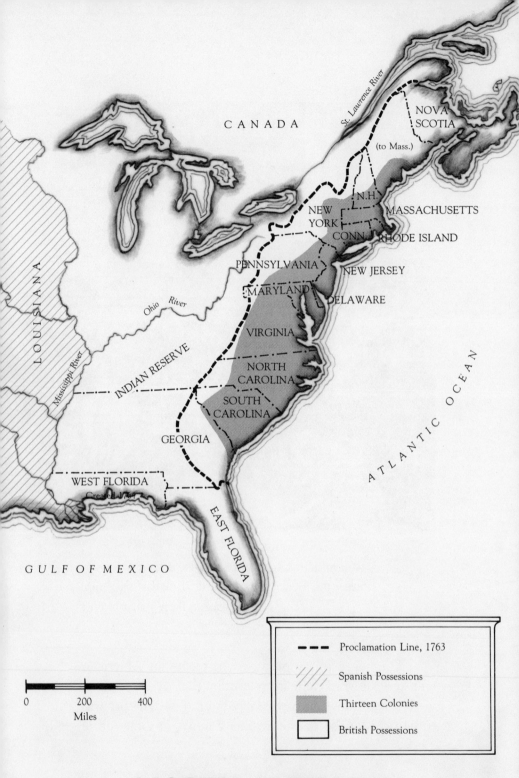

CANADA

St. Lawrence River

NOVA
SCOTIA

(to Mass.)

N.H.

NEW
YORK

MASSACHUSETTS

CONN.

RHODE ISLAND

PENNSYLVANIA

NEW JERSEY

MARYLAND

DELAWARE

LOUISIANA

Ohio River

VIRGINIA

Mississippi River

INDIAN RESERVE

NORTH
CAROLINA

SOUTH
CAROLINA

ATLANTIC OCEAN

GEORGIA

WEST FLORIDA
Created 1764

EAST
FLORIDA

GULF OF MEXICO

- - - Proclamation Line, 1763

/// Spanish Possessions

Thirteen Colonies

British Possessions

0   200   400
Miles

NORTH AMERICA
after Treaty of Paris, 1763

time. Stay on the seaboard, the colonies were told. Why? Because the war had cost far too much and London was tired of paying big bills to protect the colonists from the Indians of the interior.

This made the Americans very unhappy. Who was to run the colonies? Some authority from across the ocean or the people here on the land?

George Washington didn't worry about that now. For him there seemed nothing but happiness ahead. He was about to be married.

CHAPTER FIVE
A Planter's Life

*T*he wedding took place on January 6, 1759. George's bride was Martha Dandridge Custis, a wealthy twenty-seven-year-old widow with two children. Her husband, one of the richest planters in Virginia, had left her a large sum of money and 17,000 acres. George had danced with her at the Williamsburg balls, and liked her person and no doubt her purse. She was tiny—hardly five feet tall—with dark hair, hazel eyes, and a plump figure she dressed in elegant clothes. Not brilliant, but sensible and good-natured, the charming widow was clearly one of the most eligible ladies in the colony.

When George began courting her, what Martha saw was the very model of a military hero. An old friend, George Mercer, described him at the time as straight as an Indian, with well-developed muscles, a well-shaped head, penetrating eyes, firm chin, and a pleasing though commanding look. "In conversation," said Mercer, "he looks directly at you. His manner is composed and dignified, his movements and gestures graceful, his walk majestic."

A miniature portrait of
Martha Washington at the age of
forty, by Charles Willson Peale.
The artist's receipt for ten
guineas is shown.

May 30.th 1772. Received Ten Guineas from George Washington for drawing Mrs Washington's Picture in Miniature for the use of Mr Custis, and at his desire; —

Charles W. Peale

Martha had welcomed George's attention, pleased too that he liked her four-year-old son Jackie and her two-year-old daughter Patsy. She would create for him the happy home he had not known since his earliest years.

George slipped easily into the life of a planter, a life so different from the military. There was an enormous amount of work to be done to get Mount Vernon into shape. The place had suffered neglect in the years of his absence. He had no experience in farming. To prepare himself, he studied the best books on agriculture and farm management, including *A System of Agriculture or a Speedy Way to Get Rich*. From London he ordered long lists of household needs, not forgetting picture books and toys and trinkets for the children. He enjoyed pleasing Jackie and Patsy and all the other children in their circle.

Although still in his twenties, he acted like a patriarch, ruling over the interests of the whole Washington clan. He gave advice and aid to his brothers and sisters as well as to needy friends and acquaintances. Tobacco was his main crop. (Few knew then how deadly the weed was.) He tried to improve it to the highest quality and to acquire more land on which to raise it. Winters were filled with dozens of activities he directed: killing hogs and curing meat, sawing timber, moving buildings, repairing fences, bottling cider. As spring came, there was plowing for oats and clover, the grafting of cherry and nut trees, and experiments in sowing grass seed.

Nothing was a sure thing. He took the greatest pains imaginable, he said, but much was out of his control. When it rained endlessly, the tobacco on low ground was drowned. Or there might be a drought at the very time the tobacco plants most needed moisture. A ship carrying his tobacco went down on the coast of France. A French man-of-war captured another ship laden with his crop. Prices of the leaf dropped on the market just as the cost of clothing and supplies in London went up. Such troubles ate into his own income as well as what Martha had brought him.

Despite these setbacks, he worked steadily over the years to improve his holdings. Business always fascinated him, especially if he could profit from it. He enjoyed bargaining for land, buying a handsome new carriage, good wine, beautiful furniture. At the dock, ships discharged goods ordered to make life easier and better—perfumes, rugs, china, glass, clothing, leather bags, farm tools, feathers for Martha's headdress, saddles, spices.

Within a few years all signs of neglect were gone. Mount Vernon had the livestock, the tools, the buildings, the slaves it took to make an estate ever more valuable. George loved the planter's life. He joined investors who speculated in land enterprises in the west, and closer to home made plans to drain the Great Dismal Swamp and turn it into farmland. When his tobacco crops proved second-rate because the soil wasn't right, he turned to wheat, hemp, flax, and to weaving, milling, fisheries—anything that would make money.

And he invested more heavily in slaves. His father had left him ten, another eighteen came with Mount Vernon. In 1760 he had 49, and in 1775, 135. By this time qualms about slavery had taken hold and he had stopped buying slaves on principle. On principle he would not sell any slaves unless they gave their permission, and not one would. But earlier, he never questioned the slavery he had grown up with. At one time his household numbered over a dozen slaves, among them waiter, handyman, cook, scullion, nurse, housekeeper, weaver, carpenter. Martha trained and supervised them. Like the other Virginia masters, George treated his slaves more as property than as people. He saw to their health with the aid of a local doctor and his own infirmary. When

A *popular engraving of 1859 depicts Washington at Mount Vernon, amidst his slaves working in the fields. His stepchildren Jackie and Patsy are with him.*

a slave died he jotted down the cash value of the property he had lost. When a slave foreman ran away, George caught him and sold the "rogue" to the West Indies. He knew slaves had nothing to gain by their unpaid labor; they did as little work as they could get away with. His notion of justice was to see that none was forced to work harder than the others, and none allowed to work less hard.

He ran this sizeable enterprise efficiently, much as a military chief did his army. The chain of command ran from the top—himself as proprietor—down through managers and foremen and overseers, who were his staff officers, to the white artisans and black slaves in the ranks. He geared the complex organization to function so that the total effort would, he hoped, produce the maximum profit. His great energy and eye for detail helped make him a fine commander-in-chief.

George did not drive himself so hard that he had no time for pleasure. He enjoyed fox-hunting, fencing, shooting, and horse-racing. He liked to gamble at cards, but did not play for high stakes. Dancing—the faster the better—was a favorite diversion. A spectacle of almost any kind amused him—cockfights, puppet shows, boat races, exotic animal displays. He loved the theater and could be found down front whenever a curtain went up. He liked to breed horses and hounds, and gave them such names as Old Harry, Tipsey, Drunkard, Truelove, Sweetlips. His taste in reading ran to history and law, but his shelves held great novels and plays too. He thought of books as another way to enrich experience. Of course he smoked the tobacco he raised, buying his long-stemmed clay pipes by the gross.

The Washingtons set a lavish table. A guest might dine on terrapin and curlews, wash it down with a bottle of Madeira, then a draft of stout, followed by a Virginia cordial or a flip or toddy. George would sit up with his supper guests hour after hour—munching nuts, sipping wine, laughing over the round of jokes.

He was no Puritan, nor did he try to reform the people around him. Once he hired an able gardener, a man who liked his liquor perhaps too much. George wrote a contract with the gardener in which he agreed to give him "four dollars at Christmas with which he may be drunk four days and four nights, two dollars at Easter to effect the same purpose; two dollars also at Whitsuntide, to be drunk two days." On ordinary days, the gardener was to have "a dram in the morning, a drink of grog at dinner or at noon."

Martha was a generous hostess. In a 7-year period the Washingtons entertained some 2,000 guests. As was the custom then, people dropped in unannounced and stayed for a meal or overnight. George sometimes found half-a-dozen such guests at his door. When he entertained, he wore a plain dark coat, white waistcoat, and white silk stockings. He never wore a wig. Riding over his farms he dressed in plain blue coat, black knee breeches, and black boots.

Sundays rarely found George in church, although he was an Episcopalian. Rather than use the word "God" he preferred the term "Providence." He believed Providence was benign. How things would come out, George could not say. Man's task was to "take care to perform the part assigned to us in a way that reason and their own consciences approve of." He saw religion as a civilizing power in the secular world. He felt no prejudice against the many other faiths people believed in.

By this time George was obviously in line for public office. His military record, his wealth, his social connections, his family tradition, all made him a likely candidate. Men of his class felt they owed the community public service. That didn't mean they were above using political power to get profitable office or large grants of land. Wasn't that how the economic foundation of many a great family had been laid?

Toward the end of his frontier service, in 1758, George ran for the House of Burgesses. Although absent on duty, he was elected with the help of his influential friends—and with the customary liquid persuasion. His campaign manager served up 28 gallons of rum, 50 of rum punch, 34 of wine, 46 of beer and 2 of cider. His 396 voters drank an average quart-and-a-half of refreshments, and George happily paid the bill to join the legislature of the rich, the well-born, and the able. Here he learned his first lessons in making laws at the same time that he learned his first lessons in administration running his farms.

Elections in those times were nothing like those of today. Women, the poor, Indians, and Blacks (whether slave or free), could not vote. Only white males with a certain amount of property had the ballot. There was no secrecy at the polls. You stood up in public and announced how you were voting. There was only one polling place in each county and the two-party system had not yet been born. For local government only the burgesses and a few other officers were chosen by direct vote of the people. These practices, while not very democratic by our standards, were advanced for that time and despite their limits, many of the men elected by these means— men like George Washington—were very able men.

Williamsburg was where the legislature sat. The distance from Mount Vernon was so great—a four-day ride— that George usually attended only when local matters were being dealt with. A few days after he took his seat the burgesses voted a resolution thanking him for his military valor. He blushed as he stood up amid the roar of applause.

George did not make a big splash in his many years in the legislature. He disliked public speaking but his character and reputation gave him influence behind the scenes. "He is a modest man, but sensible, and speaks little—in action cool, like a bishop at his prayers," reported one Virginia legislator. George's popularity won him other posts of influence: county magistrate, vestryman, and then a churchwarden of his parish, and a trustee of Alexandria. By the time he was forty, he was one of the colony's most distinguished figures. In 1772 he sat for his portrait to Charles Willson Peale, the famous painter. For it he wore the uniform of a Virginia colonel. The historian Marcus Cunliffe describes the painting's impact:

> The face that gazes at us from that portrait is of a man in his prime who is at peace with the world. It is the face of a man who leads a full and active life and is thereby preserved from boredom and smugness, who is not gnawed by envy or driven on by some private demon of aggressive ambition, or kept awake at night by a load of debt, the threat of betrayal, the torment of a bad conscience. It is the face of a man who has a place in the community, near the head of things—and, one would guess, of a family man.

George was mindful of his private as well as his public obligations. If a neighbor asked for help, he could never refuse. When he was away from home for extended periods he instructed his manager "to keep up the hospitality of the house with respect to the poor." He could

Washington at forty, painted by Charles W. Peale at Mount Vernon in 1772. The earliest known portrait of Washington, it shows him in the uniform worn during the French and Indian War.

not resist a beggar's outstretched hand or a debtor unable to meet his bills, an ex-soldier who still looked to his colonel for advice, a traveler who needed a meal, or an immigrant who asked for money to bring his parents over. He gave a friend the money to send his son through college on condition that it never be mentioned.

Nor did George ask good behavior of anyone he befriended. Even when the neighborhood scapegrace who owed him large sums tried to cheat George, he did not foreclose the mortgage he held on the man's home. "Better to go laughing than crying through the rough journey of life," he once said.

He felt sympathy for sinners. Did he not give in to temptation at times? Did he always do as his conscience said? He knew that people have both weaknesses and strengths. He understood how complex and contradictory people are. Few if any are all saint or all sinner.

Sometimes his patience and tolerance were sorely tried at home. His stepson Jackie, reaching his teens, cared far more for dogs and horses and guns and fine clothes than for study. From boarding school Jackie's headmaster reported to George that he had never seen a boy so lazy and self-indulgent. The rich young idler dropped out of college, married early, and died young. Nor did his sister Patsy, far more lovable, live long. An epileptic, she died at 17. George and Martha were shaken with grief.

George often lent a hand to defenseless women whose greedy husbands used the unfair Virginia laws to cheat them out of their property. Sometimes he stood by them for years until their cases could be settled. Such sturdy friendship was rare at a time when women were treated like second-class citizens.

As for his own mother, in her early sixties she finally gave over Ferry Farm and moved into an elegant house in Fredericksburg, which George had built for her near her daughter. He did not invite her to come live with him at Mount Vernon.

The years passed with George spending most of his time taking care of Mount Vernon and his plantations. He went often to Williamsburg for the business of the legislature. Now and then there were trips to Fredericksburg, to the Dismal Swamp, to Annapolis, to friends on distant plantations. Once he made a long journey to the frontier, and canoed down the Ohio to examine land he might acquire.

Then in 1775 there comes a great change in his life. He is riding north to Boston. No longer Washington the farmer, he is now General George Washington, comander-in-chief of the thirteen American colonies in rebellion against the mother country, Great Britain.

CHAPTER SIX

The Shot Heard Round the World

*H*ow did this radical change—from country squire to revolutionary leader—occur?

For the answer, we must go back to 1763, when the Seven Years War between Britain and France ended. Britain and her American colonies had joined hands to conquer the French. Out of that victory was born a fatal conflict. Who should control the conquered lands beyond the Alleghenies?

The colonists took for granted that they would now be free to clear and settle the Mississippi Valley. In Britain, however, powerful people had other opinions. The fur traders wanted to bar the Americans from pushing across the Appalachians. They feared that if settlers entered, they would chop down the forests and drive out the Indians who caught the furry animals and sold them to the traders for export to Europe.

Not all the British agreed. Manufacturers wished to encourage the westward movement. New settlements and a growing population would mean ever bigger markets for English products. Though there might be differences over the west's future, the British did agree that the American colonies needed constant direction and control from London. And wasn't it time for the colonies to pay their share of the cost of empire? Whatever the colonies wanted, it must be subordinated to the home country's needs.

It was growing resistance to that dominance which would spark the revolution. London began to act as though the colonies were not part of Britain but its property. The first step was King George III's order forbidding Americans to move into the Mississippi Valley until further notice. The land was reserved for Indians and fur traders. The next step was the establishment of a large standing army of British troops along the American seaboard—necessary, London explained, for defense against the French and the Indians. But the French had all sailed home and most Indians were now beyond the mountains. Was this army meant for use against the colonies themselves? Many wondered.

London then decided the colonies should pay the cost of the new standing army. Britain had gone deeply into debt for the recent war. Taxes at home had climbed high. Why not make the colonies help bear the burden? So the British decided on a uniform plan for raising revenues in America. The colonies would be taxed for military protection they had not requested. Parliament had never before taxed the colonies directly; their own legislatures had done the taxing.

The proposed Stamp Act was the tax measure that upset the colonies most. It had fifty-four provisions affecting everyday business and amusements. There would be taxes on newspapers and pamphlets, on land titles,

Anno quinto

Georgii III. Regis.

CAP XII.

An Act for granting and applying certain Stamp Duties, and other Duties, in the *British* Colonies and Plantations in *America*, towards further defraying the Expences of defending, protecting, and securing the same, and for amending such Parts of the several Acts of Parliament relating to the Trade and Revenues of the said Colonies and Plantations, as direct the Manner of determining and recovering the Penalties and Forfeitures therein mentioned

WHEREAS by an Act made in the last Session of Parliament, several Duties were granted, continued, and appropriated, towards defraying the Expences of defending, protecting, and securing, the British Colonies and Plantations in America: And whereas it is just and necessary, that Provision be made for raising a further Revenue within Your Majesty's Dominions in America, towards defraying the said Expences: We, Your Majesty's most dutiful and loyal Subjects, the Commons of Great Britain in Parliament assembled,

The first page of a printed copy of the Stamp Act, imposed on the colonies by Britain in 1765

marriage licenses, playing cards, dice, almanacs, calendars. "The act managed to offend everyone," wrote one historian. "The rich, the poor, producers, consumers, the powerful, the powerless, people of commerce, people of the fields, old people making their wills, young people planning to marry, pious people going to church, ribald people going to the tavern, all of them would feel it."

No wonder the colonists did not like it. Also, the way the British acted in these matters irritated the colonists and then inflamed them. London was patronizing, obstinate, stupid at times, treating the colonists like children. At the news of the Stamp Act the colonial press grumbled loudly. But there was no violent response at first.

Then at a meeting of the Virginia legislature, a new young member—the tall, red-haired, shabbily dressed lawyer, Patrick Henry—introduced resolutions asserting that no one but the assembly had the right to lay taxes upon the colony. "Taxation without representation is tyranny!" Anyone who disagreed was an enemy of freedom. His words touched off a fiery debate. For Henry had raised a new issue—not just representation for the colonists, but home rule. The assembly toned down his language, then adopted the resolves by a majority of one.

What Virginia had done ignited debate throughout the colonies. Patrick Henry's words were reported by the press everywhere, often with even more defiant editorials. Other colonies followed Virginia's lead. Up in Boston Sam Adams, the radical leader, called upon his colony's legislature to invite delegates from all the colonies to meet for united action.

Opposition went from argument to action. Thousands pledged never to pay the taxes. The King's stamp officers were hounded, beaten, burned in effigy. Washington heard rumors that Virginians would seize and destroy the stamps. Delegates from nine colonies met in New York in the Stamp Act Congress. They published a Declaration of Rights and Grievances which most Virginians agreed with. Crowds surged on the Virginia capitol to demand the stamps not be used. The Governor heeded the warning. Protests swept the colonies.

The Stamp Act was a boomerang and Britain repealed it, in 1766. The colonists rejoiced. Some decided to ignore other British laws, especially the one requiring them to furnish supplies and quarters to royal troops. That enraged London, and when the effect of the Stamp Act repeal was to place heavier taxes on the landed gentry, they howled, and in 1767 Parliament passed the Townshend Acts, an even tougher tax program. It imposed import duties in America to be collected by Crown officials. The response was colonial refusal to import all the cherished goods from England—cloth, tools, ceramics, linen, tea—while these "odious" laws were in force.

During the gathering storm Washington was deeply concerned, but quiet. Now he wrote to a friend that "No man should scruple or hesitate a moment to use arms in defense of so valuable a blessing [freedom], on which all the good and evil of life depends." It was a major milestone on his personal road to revolution.

Washington helped prepare a list of goods Virginians should not import; the list was presented to the Assembly. When the Governor dissolved the Assembly, it adjourned to a tavern to discuss Washington's proposal, and adopted it. At the same time other colonies voted to boycott British goods. In Boston mobs rioted against the customs officials. Parliament backed down again at this broad show of resistance, and in April 1770 removed the Townshend duties for everything but tea.

In Boston a few weeks later a crowd gathered to confront British soldiers guarding the customs house. Someone threw snowballs, the soldiers panicked, an order to "Fire!" was shouted, and five Bostonians fell dead. Many others were wounded. This, the Boston Massacre, was the outcome of years of minor clashes with the unwelcome troops.

A detail of an engraving made by Paul Revere in 1768. It shows the Boston waterfront with British warships landing troops.

It was such crowd actions in the towns that stiffened the resistance movement. The crowds captured and destroyed British customs vessels. They forced officials to resign. They tore down a governor's mansion, taunted the king's soldiers. Conservative colonists who disliked what the crowds did ran great risks in opposing them. They might see their property destroyed or be tarred and feathered and driven out of town.

It was popular anger over what the British did that sparked the militancy. By itself the anger might have sputtered out. But men who called themselves Sons of Liberty—writers, small merchants, artisans—organized resistance groups in many towns and formed a network to shape public opinion and swing it into forceful action. It was they who saw that the issue of British domination was linked to a grander issue: what kind of America do we want to create? By themselves the Sons could have achieved little. But they found enormous support among the people.

Loyalists who opposed resistance to the Crown's policies suffered popular anger. Some were tarred and feathered.

Proof again of popular backing of the Sons of Liberty came in Boston when three tea ships docked at Griffin's Wharf in December 1773. Sam Adams and his well-drilled Sons of Liberty, disguising themselves as Indians, boarded the ships and threw the cargoes of tea into the harbor rather than pay duty on it. A few months later New York saw its own tea party. A crowd had turned back one tea ship and when another docked they surged aboard, ripped open the chests, dumped the tea into the water, and paraded with the empty chests to a field where they burned them.

These dramatic and illegal acts pleased many. George Washington thought they might push the British to even worse acts of oppression. When outraged London retaliated by closing the port of Boston and removing the charter of Massachusetts, he said these "intolerable acts . . . exhibited an unexampled testimony of the most despotic system of tyranny that was ever practised in a free government." Now it was every colonial's absolute duty to oppose that tyranny.

The Virginia legislators denounced the closing of the Boston port "as a most violent and dangerous attempt to destroy the constitutional liberty and rights of all British Americans." Then they called for delegates from all the colonies to meet and consider how best to secure their constitutional rights. Washington helped shape these decisions. He had thought that somehow differences with the mother country would be worked out. But he and the others now took the revolutionary step of proclaiming a common cause and proposing an annual Congress that implied America was ready to govern her own affairs. If Britain continued to deny the colonies their fundamental rights, then complete separation would be justified.

And what could follow? A revolutionary American political union? A major move in that direction was taken when the Virginians called for linking together the Committees of Correspondence to promote solidarity among the colonies. The committees began exchanging information about Britain's maneuvers and developing joint action to resist them.

As the crisis intensified, loyalty to the Crown diminished. More and more voices cried that the colonies themselves were the final judges of the liberties they claimed. No longer would they look to the mother country for decision on constitutional issues. What then, or who, could settle such issues? Something brand new: a congress of the colonies.

On September 5, 1774 the First Continental Congress met in Philadelphia. Washington was one of the seven men chosen to represent his colony. The Virginians knew they could count on him to do the right thing. As the delegates met, they were angered by the news that British troops had occupied Boston.

This was Washington's first chance to get to know so many leaders from all the colonies. He listened closely to the speeches and resolutions on the floor of Congress, to the talk in the taverns and lodgings. He took political temperatures, finding some men hot, some cool, some lukewarm. And he read carefully the newspapers and pamphlets debating the difficult issues before the Congress. While he did not make speeches, he impressed the delegates in private talks as a man of integrity. They respected his military reputation and his intense concern with the problems of the whole continent, north and south.

In six weeks the Congress reached agreement. It

devised a Continental Association whose aim was to shut off trade with Britain completely. Local committees would be set up to see that the boycott was enforced. In a Declaration of Rights, the Americans gave notice to Britain that the colonies would no longer be bound by Parliament's laws or the king's will when it infringed on their liberties. The Congress demanded repeal of all the offensive acts passed by Parliament since 1763, and scheduled a second Congress for the spring of 1775.

A long process that had begun ten years before had now climaxed in a revolutionary program. Independence was not yet demanded, only freedom to decide their own affairs. The Congress told the world America had grown into a mature society with a will of its own and a future it meant to shape for itself.

What would the British do? The Congress knew war was possible. If it came, the British would have to start it. And if they struck, the colonies would fight back. When Washington reached home, he found young men already organizing military companies and drilling with guns. All over the colonies people were preparing for war. Washington met with other colony leaders to plan what Virginia could do. Early in the spring, a Virginian assembly approved the decisions of the Continental Congress and considered military action. Patrick Henry took the floor to argue that there was only one way Americans could sustain their liberty. "We must fight!" he cried out. "Is life so dear, or peace so sweet, as to be purchased at the price of chains and slavery? Forbid it, Almighty God! I know not what course others may take; but as for me, give me liberty or give me death!" The delegates voted to organize the colony for defense, levying taxes to buy arms, ammunition, and equipment. Washington was chosen to develop military plans and elected a delegate to the Second Continental Congress.

Just then the news that many had dreaded—and others had hoped for—arrived from the north. Blood had been spilled in Massachusetts. The king's forces and the colonials had clashed. A British general in Boston had sent a thousand troops to seize a store of munitions which the colonists had hidden at Concord. But the alarm had been given. At dawn on April 19, the marching redcoats came upon a barrier of fifty Minutemen in the village of Lexington, ten miles northwest of Boston. Shots rang out; eight Americans were killed, ten more wounded.

A famous picture of the Battle of Lexington, drawn by Ralph Earle and engraved by Amos Doolittle in 1775

The British then marched on to Concord where they searched the town for hidden military supplies. Volunteers flocked in and musket fire was exchanged at the bridge over the Concord River. The Concord fight— "the shot heard round the world"—had taken about three minutes. Two Concord men and three redcoats fell dead. The British panicked and ran. When they started back to Boston the Americans, hidden behind barns and trees along the road, picked them off by the score.

The British had struck the expected blow and the colonials had proved they would resist. Couriers rushed to all the colonies with the news. Early in May, Washington rode north to Philadelphia to attend the Second Continental Congress. At Baltimore he was asked to review the town's volunteer companies. The wealthy planter was now looked upon as a soldier, one of the few experienced military officers the colonies could claim.

When the Congress opened, Washington was assigned to head a group to respond to colonial requests for military aid and advice. Action came faster than expected. Vermont frontiersmen led by Ethan Allen seized Fort Ticonderoga on Lake Champlain, a strategic military post rich in military supplies. A few days later the Congress decided they had better start raising an army "for the preservation of our liberties." Washington chaired a committee to figure out how to supply the colonies with their military needs.

The majority of delegates still hoped to force the British to give America a decent place inside the Empire. But Washington had little faith in reconciliation. As he prepared defense plans he took to wearing his red and blue uniform from the French and Indian War. It was a signal to the Congress that it was time to fight. He did not welcome war; its tragic nature saddened him. "Unhappy it is," he wrote, "to reflect that a brother's sword has been sheathed in a brother's breast and that the once-happy and peaceful plains of America are either to be drenched with blood or inhabited by slaves. Sad alternative! But can a virtuous man hesitate in his choice?"

Congress asked Washington to estimate the war funds it would need to raise as the troops of nearby colonies moved up to Boston to aid in its defense. This was the beginning of a continental army, an army that needed a commander in chief. On June 15, 1775 the name of George Washington was proposed. He was unanimously elected.

CHAPTER SEVEN

Times That Try Men's Souls

Now he was in full command of an army fighting a revolution.

It was not an honor Washington had looked for. He had quit the army seventeen years before to seek a private life, a life of peace and plenty. What could the leader of a revolution expect if he lost? Surely no mercy, only the destruction of everything he had created so lovingly. And perhaps the hangman's noose.

When he accepted appointment as general and commander in chief, he rose and said to the Congress: "I feel great distress from a consciousness that my abilities and military experience may not be equal to the extensive and important trust. However, as the Congress desires, I will enter upon the momentous duty, and exert every power I possess in their service, and for the support of the glorious cause. . . . But, lest some unlucky event should happen unfavorable to my reputation, I beg it may be remembered by every gentleman in the room, that I this day declare with the utmost sincerity, I do not think myself equal to the command I am honored with. . . ."

*Washington taking command of the
Continental Army, Cambridge, 1775*

He refused to accept any pay, asking only that his
expenses be met.

He had good reason to doubt his qualifications. What
were they? Five years in a militia company, no experience
in tactics, except in the wilderness. He had never formed
large strategic plans. He knew nothing of artillery, of
cavalry, of supply, of the care of casualties. Nor had he
ever commanded any large body of troops. Discipline was
what he had learned, discipline as the backbone of any
army. He had been a dashing officer, eager for action.
Surely that spirit was needed now—but more, much more

than that. Amid the trials to come, he would show he had other great qualities—patience, pity, coolness, endurance, and a rocklike will. His very presence radiated authority. In a sprawling net of colonies facing the great test of a struggle for freedom and for survival as a new nation, his character would be decisive.

His military schooling was minor, and he had thought or read little about war since those youthful years. His political schooling, however, as a Virginia legislator, would prove invaluable in his dealing with Congress. He had learned how to work with legislative committees, when to compromise and when to be stubborn. And most of all, he had learned that respect and frankness in public affairs earned good will and trust.

America was up against the greatest odds. It seemed foolish to challenge Britain, the world's richest nation, with a population five times that of America. What could the infant nation do against the world's greatest military and naval power?

Still, Britain had serious handicaps. The war was expensive, and unpopular at home. Britain's troops were scattered around the globe. Soldiers had to be hired from foreign princes, and transported, with supplies, across 3,000 miles of rough seas. Communications were slow and uncertain. Many British officers were poorly qualified; they had bought, not earned, their commissions. Nor were the politicians who devised strategy much better. America had no great centers of population and production that British troops could wipe out. To win, Britain had to destroy Washington's evasive army or else occupy the vast stretches of America. How could an army trained under radically different conditions fight troops that could hide in woods and mountains and swamps and spring from ambush when they liked?

The Revolutionary forces, on the other hand, were miserable enough to discourage any general. There was no central authority to run the war. Congress had to appeal to the states for troops; the states passed the requisition on to their counties, which enlisted men only for six-month terms. The soldiers elected their own officers, often refused to take discipline, might mutiny if asked to fight too far from home, and sometimes deserted "almost by regiments," in Washington's words. Several times he appealed for a centralized draft, but each time the Congress only rebuked him. Finally Congress offered bounties of money and land to men who would enlist in the Continental service for the duration. But the lure was less than the individual states offered to their own militia for shorter service within their own boundaries. The Continental army never grew large but at least it gave Washington a seasoned core of regulars.

As the long war wore on—it lasted eight years— men who could afford it saved themselves from service by hiring a substitute or paying a substantial fine. Some towns ignored conscription orders and hired men to fill the state quotas. By 1777, the ranks were made up largely of the poor.

Supply and pay of the army were wretched from the early campaigns to the very end. Troops were always short of guns and ammunition. When the men were paid— and often they were not—it was in Continental paper dollars, worth almost nothing. Often the men were left without uniforms, boots, or blankets. Only Washington's

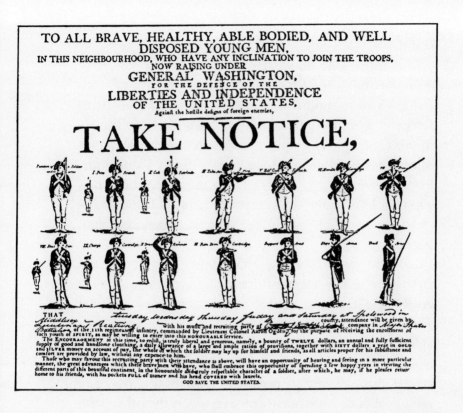

One of Washington's recruiting posters, urging patriots to join his army. Would the appeal cause you to sign up?

sheer doggedness could keep some kind of army in the field under such conditions.

The profiteering and the incompetence he saw sickened Washington. In a private letter he spoke of the "dirty, mercenary spirit" and "want of virtue" people displayed in seeking personal advantage from the war. If he had foreseen all this, he said, "no consideration upon this earth should have induced me to accept this command."

Although he could rely on some senior officers of great ability, several lacked the basic qualities of leadership. Many found their duties so difficult, and themselves so worn out, that they put aside their obligation to the country and simply quit. By contrast Washington himself served the eight long years without a single furlough, leave, or even day's rest. An amazing record when you recall his many illnesses before he took command—smallpox, typhoid, dysentery, malaria, tubercular pleurisy.

What made Washington's burden heavier was the fact that the war against Britain was at the same time a cruel, devastating civil war, a war of American against American. Historians say that a third or even half of the colonists were opposed to the revolution. Undeniably, laborers, artisans, farmers, small merchants, the common people, were strong patriots. But perhaps a majority of the upper class were openly or secretly on the other side. Every colony had its people loyal to the king. Thousands returned to England or fled to Canada when the fighting started. Thousands more joined the royal troops or native Tory bands that raided for loot or vengeance.

The Loyalists or Tories scornfully labelled the patriots as lower class and uneducated. They sounded one common theme—that all men are *not* created equal, some are better than others. The patriots, on their side, accused the Loyalists of burning towns, ravaging the countryside, discouraging enlistment, harboring deserters, spying for the enemy. One Philadelphia editor cried out, "Who wish to see us conquered, to see us slaves, to see us hewers of wood and drawers of water? The Tories!" Washington himself came to believe the Tories were capable of almost any crime to defeat the American cause.

So the moment he took command, Washington waded into a sea of troubles. His duty was to keep Britain from destroying the revolution. He had small hopes that his army would grow strong enough to win on the battlefield. No, the war would have to be won in the minds of Americans. If enough of them held out long enough for American freedom, then the British could never regain the colonies.

The first scene of action was New England. Washington hurried to Boston to join the militia besieging the British troops in the town. He made his headquarters in the village of Cambridge two weeks after the British had taken Breed's Hill (miscalled Bunker Hill) in a battle that cost them ten times the casualties suffered by the Americans. Washington sent an expedition to Canada under Colonel Benedict Arnold to seize Quebec and win over the Canadian provinces. He urged an assault upon the British in Boston, but when Arnold's mission failed, his council of war voted down the proposal.

Hating to do nothing, he was forced to sit out the winter of 1775–76. Perhaps he was amused to learn that Yankee parents were naming their newborn sons after him. As the New Year opened, a bombshell exploded in print. Tom Paine published his great pamphlet, *Common Sense*. A poor English immigrant, Paine had settled in Philadelphia only two years before, siding with the radicals. He advocated an immediate declaration of independence, and quickly sold 500,000 copies, creating America's first best-seller. His passionate words ignited

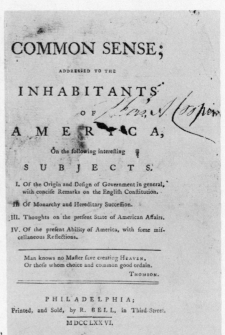

Portrait of Tom Paine and the title page of his 1776 pamphlet, Common Sense. *His powerful message calling for immediate independence was greeted by Washington as "sound and unanswerable."*

the minds of the farmers and mechanics. He made vividly clear what they were against—the British system itself, with its monarchy and inequality. Americans, he said, you can show the world how to break free of the tyranny of kings and nobles. You best know your own wants and needs, and you are best able to rule yourselves. This is your chance, independence is what you are fighting for. "Sound doctrines and unanswerable reasoning," said Washington.

Early in March, Washington's troops seized the heights commanding Boston and its harbor, and forced the British to end the siege and sail away north to Nova Scotia. With them fled 1,100 Tory refugees, many from the wealthiest families of the colony. Massachusetts and northern New England were free of the redcoats for the rest of the war. The British strategy was to regroup in Halifax, in order to invade New York State and capture New York City.

Shortly after the victory in Boston, the Second Continental Congress began to cut the last ties with Britain. It sent diplomats to France to seek men and money from Britain's old enemy. It opened American ports to all nations, ending Britain's control over commerce. And it advised the colonies to set up new governments to replace the royal officials. Independence was but one step away.

On July 2 that final step was taken. Congress voted for a resolution of independence introduced a month before by the Virginian Richard Henry Lee. It was no easy thing to do, this breaking of emotional, political, economic ties with the mother country. That's why it came a whole year after the bloodshed of Lexington and Concord. On July 4 the Congress adopted the Declaration of Independence prepared by a committee but actually written by Thomas Jefferson.

The opening lines of Jefferson's rough draft
of the Declaration of Independence

John Trumbull's painting of the scene at the Continental Congress in Philadelphia on July 4, 1776, when the Declaration of Independence was adopted. Standing at the left of the table are the five members appointed to draft it. Thomas Jefferson, who actually wrote it, is standing with his hands on the document.

Its aim was to justify a war already being fought, and to enlist international support for it. The ideas can be traced back to the Scottish thinkers of the earlier eighteenth century. They believed that governments exist to preserve self-evident human rights, such as the rights to life and liberty. If a government no longer protects those rights, and in fact does just the opposite— endangering the safety and happiness of the people— then it is no longer a true government but a tyranny. And to resist such tyranny with force is then justified.

After an appeal to the world's public opinion, the Declaration states high principles: "that all men are created equal; that they are endowed by their creator with certain unalienable rights; that among these are life, liberty and the pursuit of happiness." The second part aims to prove that Americans have great cause to rebel by spelling out "a long train of abuses" that demonstrate the king's intention to reduce them to slavery. The final section proclaims America's independence.

The belief that any sovereign people's most important right is to rule itself on whatever terms it may choose was not new then. And today everyone would agree with it, though a great many nations prefer to ignore it. The five words "all men are created equal" would become the very core of the American conscience. Though interpreted in many different ways, the celebrated words can never be erased or forgotten.

Washington, now in New York, had the Declaration read to his army. He hoped, he told them, that "this important event will serve as a fresh incentive to every officer and soldier to act with fidelity and courage, as knowing that now the peace and safety of his country depends, under God, solely on the success of our arms."

With an inexperienced army half the size of Britain's 35,000 men, Washington had no hope of holding New York. But he meant to make the British bleed for every inch of ground. Late in August he met the British on Long Island in the first pitched battle he had ever directed. He was outclassed and defeated but managed to evacuate his troops across the East River into Manhattan. The British commander, General Howe, forced him out of the city and chased him up the Hudson valley. Until the war's end the British would hold New York.

It was a grievous and humiliating loss. Many of Washington's officers were "not worth the bread they eat," he said bitterly, and the men were cowardly and undisciplined. Their short-term enlistments ended, the militia melted away. Washington issued General Orders to reduce straggling, plundering, malingering, desertion. In a letter to Congress he pleaded for great speed in securing long-term enlistments with better pay and supply.

How he kept his resolve in command of so weak and dispirited an army is a tribute to his patience and faith. Unable to hold his forts on the Hudson, he crossed to the New Jersey side. He moved south with the redcoats snapping at his heels. He got his army over the Delaware River near Trenton when he learned that Hessian troops had entered the town. They were among the many thousand mercenaries George III had hired from several German princes to fill out the ranks of the British.

Washington's army numbered only 3,000 men, shivering in the December frost. In that almost hopeless moment Tom Paine sat down in the gloomy American camp to write *The Crisis*. "These are the times that try men's souls. . . ." Again Paine was able to stiffen crumbling morale. Only a desperate move could prevent disaster. Late on Christmas night, in the midst of a sleet storm that whipped his boats, Washington ferried troops and artillery across the Delaware. At daybreak they surprised the Hessians, who were sleeping off their Christmas revels at Trenton. The Americans stormed the town, killed the Hessian commander, and took some 900 of his men prisoner.

A victory at last—a lucky one, but a victory. In the worst hour Washington had won his finest success, without losing a single American life. He congratulated the troops on their "gallant and spirited" attack and, ordering rum for all hands, asked how anyone could think now of "abandoning the cause of liberty and their country."

Enlistments were up in a few days: would any soldiers stay on? With no authority to do it, he offered a bounty of ten dollars to anyone who would add six weeks to his term. He had learned that money, if nothing else, might appeal to them. He explained to the troops "in the most affectionate manner" why they were needed. His appeal and the bonus induced about half of them to stay.

Again Washington moved. He struck the British at Princeton, beating three regiments, and forced Lord Cornwallis to drop back to protect his supply base. Washington then moved up to Morristown, and went into winter quarters. (Armies in those days usually campaigned in the warmer months, then encamped for the winter.)

A brilliant campaign had recovered New Jersey in just ten days and made his soldiers feel they had a real chance to win. Desertions dropped to a rate the general could live with.

*After crossing the Delaware River and beating
the British at Trenton, Washington won another
victory at Princeton. The retaking of New Jersey
heartened the country and made the American
troops believe victory was possible.*

In London, news of the defeats in New Jersey blasted
British hopes of ending the war quickly. A three-pronged
attack was planned to conquer the state of New York.
Once it was in British hands, the country and the rebellion would be cut in two. Could Washington spoil
that strategy?

CHAPTER EIGHT

The World Turned Upside Down

Three British spearheads headed for their target—New York State. With a massive army of regulars, Hessians, Canadians, and Indians, General John Burgoyne marched south toward Albany from the St. Lawrence, by way of Lake Champlain and the Hudson. Another army of mostly Loyalists and Indians, under Colonel St. Leger, headed westward from Lake Ontario through the Mohawk Valley to meet Burgoyne at Albany. And General Howe, comfortable among the fashionable Tories in New York, was prepared to give support to both armies at the right moment.

Nothing worked as planned. It usually doesn't, in war. Howe decided he could end the war by taking Philadelphia. So he left part of his men in New York to help Burgoyne and shipped the larger part to Chesapeake Bay.

Before St. Leger got halfway to Albany he was turned back in a bloody battle at Oriskany. Burgoyne—an amusing playwright known as "Gentleman Johnny"—was slowed by his great string of baggage wagons. They got tangled up in the forests between Lake Champlain and the Hudson. American frontiersmen had felled hundreds of trees across his line of march and riflemen harassed him all along the way. Neither St. Leger nor Howe were where they should be to help him. Short of provisions, Burgoyne sent his plumed and sabered troops to seize American supplies at Bennington; they were attacked by General John Stark and his Green Mountain sharpshooters and almost all of them were killed or taken prisoner.

Burgoyne decided to press on to Albany on the west side of the Hudson. Brought to bay at Saratoga by General Horatio Gates, he was beaten decisively. In mid-October what was left of his army—5,700 men—laid down their arms. They were marched to Boston and shipped back to England, pledged not to serve again in the war against the Americans.

The victory at Saratoga gave the war a decisive turn. When the French heard of Burgoyne's surrender, they decided to recognize the independence of the United States and to enter into an alliance with her. Meanwhile Washington was nervously trying to anticipate General Howe's intentions. When the British fleet sailed out of New York harbor in late July its goal seemed to be Philadelphia, or was it Charleston? Or perhaps Howe would double back and move up the Hudson. The waiting was torment. Finally the British were sighted going up the Chesapeake. It meant they would then march overland to Philadelphia. Howe's plan was to force Washington into battle and destroy his army. If the British could take the American capital it would cripple the rebellion and, Howe expected, end it.

Washington paraded his ragged troops through Philadelphia where the Congress sat, and headed for a defensive stand behind the Brandywine River. But Howe outflanked him on the left and came in behind the American lines. The Continentals were beaten but Washington led a successful rearguard action which enabled most of his men to escape. Howe tried again and again to tempt the Americans into decisive battle. Washington marched here and there and everywhere, refusing the bait, hoping for an opening that would give him a better crack at the British. Finally Howe outmaneuvered Washington and slipped into Philadelphia as easily as if he owned it. Washington had lost the largest American city. It was even more humiliating than his forced departure from New York. Congress fled to Lancaster and then to York where it set up again its shaky government.

With winter coming on, Washington yearned for a major blow against the British before the snows would make action impossible. Lord Cornwallis held Philadelphia with 3,000 men. Another 5,000 British were encamped in the suburb of Germantown. Washington thought he would try for another Trenton victory, but a bigger one. He called in troops from as far off as the Hudson forts, amassing 8,000 Continentals and 3,000 militia. On the night of October 3, 1777, he began an intricate movement toward Howe's camp. The battle began at dawn in a heavy and welcome fog. With the first thrust, the British began to fall back, and Washington ordered more regiments forward. What a rare feeling to find his army forcing back the British! And then his complex plan fell apart. Troops foundered in the thick fog and at one point began shooting down one another. Some columns didn't show up at all, others moved in late. As several brigades forged ahead, the advance detachment which had reached Howe's encampment began running back. The soldiers moving up with Washington stopped dead at the sight, then they too turned and ran. Washington yelled for them to halt and tried to turn them around but panic had gripped them. Near-victory in the Battle of Germantown had turned into a rout.

Washington's casualties, including prisoners taken, were nearly 1,100, twice those of the British. Ever confident of the cause, he felt disappointed, but not defeated. Then came the great news of Burgoyne's surrender at Saratoga. Washington withdrew to the northeast and settled into winter quarters at Valley Forge.

Two weeks after Burgoyne surrendered, a fast ship under Captain John Paul Jones cleared Boston to carry the news to Benjamin Franklin, America's representative in France. Louis XVI saw Burgoyne's defeat as his chance to enter the war openly on the side of the Americans. (Spain would soon come in too, and then Holland.) The fighting of a few thousand men in the north woods had made a critical turn in world history.

France came in not because the king loved freedom but because he hoped to weaken the British and gain back some of the empire he had lost. French liberals like the young Marquis de Lafayette were eager to join America in its fight against tyranny. Now America could count on great European powers for help, whatever their motives.

France had already been secretly supplying the rebels with arms and provisions. Lafayette, early in 1777, had

Lake Superior

Quebec ✸

Montreal · St. Lawrence R.

MASS.

Crown Point
Fort Ticonderoga △

NEW
HAMPSHIRE

Lake Huron

Fort
Stanwix ✸ Saratoga ✸ Lexington ✸ Bunker
                                        Hill
Lake Ontario   Oriskany ✸ Concord ✸   Boston
Lake Michigan   Bennington MASS.
            NEW YORK
Fort Detroit △   West Point ·   CONN.   R.I.
Lake Erie   Stony ✸ White Plains ✸   Newport
Allegheny R.   Point △ Morristown · Long Island ✸
            PENNSYLVANIA Princeton ✸ New York ✸
Fort Pitt △   Valley Forge △   Monmouth ✸
                 Brandywine ✸ Trenton ✸
                         Germantown ✸
                         Philadelphia ·
              MARYLAND
                      DEL.

Cahokia ✸   Vincennes ✸   Ohio R

Kaskaskia ✸   VIRGINIA

Mississippi River   Richmond ·
                    Williamsburg ·   Yorktown ✸

                         Edenton ·
             Guilford ✸
             Courthouse

             Kings Mountain ✸   NORTH CAROLINA
                    · Charlotte
   Cowpens ✸
                    Camden ✸
             SOUTH CAROLINA
     Augusta ·
     GEORGIA   Charleston ✸

     Savannah ✸
          △

ATLANTIC OCEAN

The Thirteen Colonies

✸ Battles

△ Forts

0   Miles   200

BATTLES of the REVOLUTION

sailed to America with a dozen French officers to place themselves under Washington's command. France had held off giving official aid until America could prove it had a chance to win. The news of Saratoga satisfied the king's ministers. They sat down with American diplomats to sign treaties of alliance and commerce and both sides pledged not to cease fighting until Britain acknowledged American independence. "No event was ever received with more heartfelt joy," said Washington. Looking back, we can see this was the turning point of the war.

News of Saratoga changed Britain's attitude too. A bill for reconciliation with America was passed in Parliament in February of 1778; it granted the Americans all they had asked for before they broke away from the empire. But as Washington said, "Nothing short of independence can possibly do." And this the British would not grant.

Months before Britain's too-late gesture, the Americans had taken another major step to self-government. A plan to confederate the colonies had been prepared by a committee of Congress back in July 1776. The Congress debated the Articles of Confederation for a year. In November 1777 the thirteen articles were formally adopted and sent to the states for their approval. (It would take over three years for complete ratification to come from the states. The delay was caused by Maryland's refusal to ratify until the states claiming western lands ceded them to the U.S.)

While Howe snuggled down in warm Philadelphia, Washington's army stood watch eighteen miles northwest at Valley Forge. The villages close to Philadelphia were

*An early engraving of General Washington
making the rounds of his troops wintering
under terribly harsh conditions at Valley
Forge. Many froze and starved in dugouts.*

so crowded with refugees there were no roofs to shelter soldiers. They camped on 1,500 acres along the Schuylkill, shivering under canvas for many long weeks before they could move into crude huts built of trees from the nearby forest. The commissariat was so callous and inept that men starved, froze, and died for lack of food, clothing, blankets, medicine. And Congress did little to help.

The winter wasn't the worst those parts had seen, but that was poor comfort for the 8,000 men. They used their hats for shoes and made leggings out of straw and paper. One of three was unfit for duty: puking, coughing, spitting, wheezing, down with the fever or the itch or the trots and unable to breathe free for the intolerable stench. Had the British thought to pursue them, their poor carcasses would have littered the fields.

No furloughs were granted for ranks above captain. Officers could leave only by resigning or deserting. "Resigning has become epidemical," Washington wrote, as he watched his Virginia line lose ninety officers in that way, among them "six colonels as good as any in the service." Untold numbers of the men ran away, to be hanged if caught. No one who knew what that camp was like was surprised, least of all General Washington. The wonder was, he thought, that so many stayed.

Still, there were flashes of good news that cut through the gloom. Frederick the Great of Prussia said the odds for the Americans winning were 100 to 1 in their favor. Baron Friedrich von Steuben, a veteran of Prussian wars, joined Washington at Valley Forge to drill the troops. And as the ordeal of that winter dragged to an end, Count d'Estaing sailed for America with twelve French warships and many French regiments.

Outwardly, Washington seemed to be unshaken. His men had not mutinied; they had done better than their officers expected, so great was their confidence in Washington. He had for a short time the comfort of Martha's presence. She would spend part of every winter with him, even here at Valley Forge. She reminded him of far-off Mount Vernon, now in charge of a cousin. In his letters home he set aside his military worries to ask how many lambs had been born in the spring, or to propose an agricultural experiment, or a repair of the house. But most of the time he was busy with the thousand details of the crises he had to face. He wrote endlessly to Congress and his officers in the field—prodding, reminding, criticizing, suggesting, explaining, demanding, complaining. If only everyone did his part and did it well, his labors would be much reduced. But he had too great a conscience and too powerful a will to win to let anything slip notice.

The French alliance led Howe's successor, Sir Henry Clinton, to abandon Philadelphia, as the British had given up Boston only two years before. Clinton knew the forts on the Delaware were not strong enough to protect the city against the feared French fleet. He led his army of 17,000 men on a march through New Jersey, toward New York. A moral victory, Washington thought, as he broke camp at Valley Forge and chased after Clinton. On June 28, a fiercely hot Sunday, the Americans under General Charles Lee met Clinton at Monmouth. Lee badly mismanaged the attack and Clinton drove him back. Washington appeared just in time to organize a defense that stopped the British. The army's new training under von Steuben showed results. The confused and scattered troops obeyed Washington's commands at once. Lafayette said Washington "seemed to arrest fortune with one glance. His presence stopped the retreat. His calm and deportment are all calculated to inspire the highest degree of enthusiasm. I had never beheld so superb a man." The British had lost 1,200 men, four times more than the Americans.

That night the redcoats stole away and headed for New York. Washington moved northward, crossed the Hudson and took up a position in White Plains above New York City.

The British decided to concentrate action in the southern states. They believed many Loyalists there were eager to fight alongside them. They captured Savannah and overran all of Georgia, restoring the royal governor. Then, in December 1779, Clinton sailed from New York with an army of 5,000 men to conquer South Carolina. In May 1780 he took Charleston and with it some 5,000 American soldiers. He had knocked out almost the entire American army south of the Potomac.

Both in Georgia and South Carolina the British and their Loyalist allies treated the patriots ruthlessly. They burned houses and barns, killed cattle, destroyed crops, and threw rebel sympathizers into prison camps. Clinton returned to New York, leaving Lord Cornwallis with 8,000 men in command in the South. Washington felt he had to stand watch over Clinton in New York and sent what troops he could spare to the South. Over the general's opposition, Congress picked Horatio Gates to take command in South Carolina. But the victor at Saratoga was badly beaten by Cornwallis at Camden, and in August General Greene was defeated by the British at Guilford Court House. The southern states seemed lost to the patriot cause.

But as Cornwallis moved confidently toward an expected victory, a fresh resistance rose up. Several regiments of American backwoodsmen wiped out 1,200 Loyalists at King's Mountain near the northern border of South Carolina. That crushing defeat terrified the British and the Loyalists while it stirred up patriotic fervor throughout the southern backcountry. Guerrilla bands struck the British at every turn. Cornwallis could make no headway against their superior hit-and-run tactics.

In the winter of 1779–80 the condition of Washington's small army, encamped at Morristown, New Jersey, was even worse than it had been at Valley Forge. Supplies failed to arrive, rations had to be savagely cut. The soldiers seethed with anger. One colonial said, "I damn my country as void of gratitude!" How could the Congress and the states let their own army starve? Washington feared mutiny at any moment. In May, two Connecticut regiments came out of their huts with their guns to demand full rations and all the back pay long overdue them, or they would go home. Luckily Pennsylvania troops were able to curb them and supplies soon came in. Washington wrote Congress that the tragic condition of his army gave him "infinitely more concern than anything that has ever hapened." To a friend he confided, "I have almost ceased to hope." News that Charleston had fallen made him see only calamity ahead. When he asked the states to send him 17,000 militia, their call produced 30 men. So desperate was the army's condition that Washington feared the French would see how helpless the Americans were and sail back home.

In July the French fleet anchored at Newport and placed 5,000 troops in the town, under command of Count de Rochambeau. He was told to pretend to take orders from Washington. He took care to keep his troops separate from the Americans. He was appalled to find how small and weak his ally was. Even taken together the two armies were not yet strong enough to do what Washington wanted most of all—to attack New York. Maybe next year, they told themselves.

Meanwhile Washington rode up to West Point to inspect the fortress and visit with the commander he had appointed, his much-admired protegé, General Benedict Arnold. He arrived to find Arnold strangely absent. Hours later a messenger came, with a packet of papers. Washington opened them and cried out, "Arnold has betrayed us! Whom can we trust now?" The chance capture of Major John André, a British spy Arnold had been secretly working with, revealed that Arnold had plotted to turn over West Point to the British. It was one of the worst emotional shocks of Washington's life. André was hanged as a spy, while the traitor Arnold escaped to join the British. Luckily Arnold was a rare case; treason was never a really serious danger to the Revolution.

The Americans enjoyed some minor victories on land, and at sea Captain John Paul Jones and other naval officers won many small encounters. But these did little to affect the outcome of the war. That would come to climax in the South. American victories there had confined Cornwallis to the seacoast, just where he had started from a year before. Orders came to him from General Clinton in New York to send up reinforcements. Clinton feared Washington's army and the fleet of the French Admiral de Grasse would combine to recapture New York. Cornwallis obeyed, reluctantly, and gathered what was left of his army behind fortifications on the Virginia peninsula of Yorktown.

The French told Washington that their fleet would be able to give him help, and he moved quickly to catch Cornwallis in a trap. The French ships would sail up from the West Indies to Chesapeake Bay and cut off any attempt by the British to relieve Cornwallis by sea. And a joint force of Americans and French could close in on him by land.

Rochambeau's army joined Washington's north of Manhattan in July 1781. When they dined together the French were startled by the informality of the American officers. They sat for hours at table, cracking nuts, telling jokes, and offering ribald toasts while Washington leaned back and enjoyed it all. Observing him in camp, the French saw that all his men looked upon him as both father and friend.

In August preparations began for the long hard march 450 miles south to meet de Grasse in Virginia. Washington was deeply worried by the uncertainties of the strategy. Suppose storms at sea or change of French orders kept the fleet from arriving? And what if Cornwallis got wind of the plan and escaped the trap by marching inland? And wouldn't Clinton notice the departure of the two armies and guess their destination? To throw him off, Washington leaked misinformation he knew would reach the ears of spies. De Grasse was said to be sailing north to help attack New York. Engineers began to lay out what looked like a major camp in New Jersey. Clinton was fooled, and the armies reached the Delaware before he guessed the truth.

Clinton ordered the British fleet to sail at once from New York, and head for Chesapeake Bay to intercept the French. De Grasse was debarking 3,000 French troops at Jamestown when the British fleet appeared. The French ships badly disabled the British in a battle at sea, and then deployed across Chesapeake Bay, barring it from any move by the British. In their battered condition they could do nothing but return to New York, leaving Cornwallis to his fate at Yorktown.

Washington was mightily relieved; this part of his plan had gone beautifully. Systematic as ever, he turned to problems of supply and leadership to ensure the siege of Cornwallis's troops would not be spoiled by any attempt to escape.

On September 28 Washington began the siege, moving the Allied troops up. For the first time he enjoyed two military advantages commanders pray for. With his combined force of 16,000 American and French troops, he had superiority in manpower, and he could count on excellent officers. Two days later Cornwallis abandoned his outer line of fortifications. This enabled the Allies to bring up their siege guns to hammer at his inner lines. After heavy firing, part of the British line was taken. A British counterattack failed, and Cornwallis felt his position was now hopeless. When a storm disrupted his desperate plan to escape across the York River, he decided to surrender. On October 19 his entire army of 7,250 regulars, together with 850 sailors, 244 cannon, and a large supply of military stores fell to the Allies. The bands played "The World Turned Upside Down" as the British regiments marched through the American and French ranks to lay down their arms.

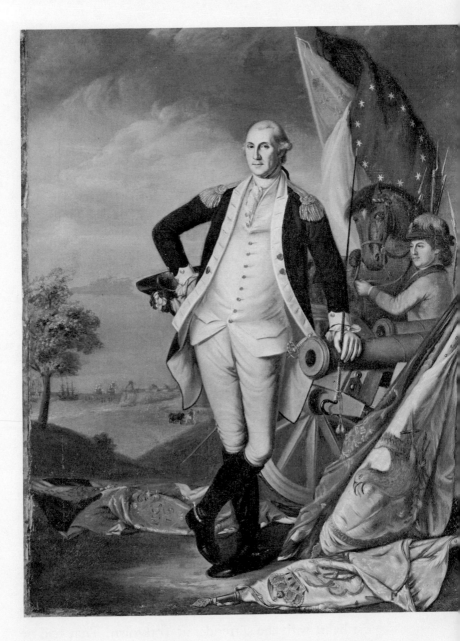

Peale's portrait of Washington at Yorktown

For George Washington it was a glorious climax. His Continentals had performed superbly in this final siege. The world cheered his victory; even the British admired his leadership. But the war would drag on for another year, and the army, not knowing when or how it would end, became restless and bad-tempered and rebellious. They feared Congress would forget every promise of money or land or pension after the war was over. When many officers threatened armed revolt, Washington met with them to hear their grievances. He begged them not to do anything that would "lessen the dignity or sully the glory" they had demonstrated to the world. Then, taking out a letter on this point to read to them, he paused. "Gentlemen," he said, as he fumbled with his new spectacles, "you must pardon me. I have grown gray in your service and now find myself growing blind." Those words reached their deepest feelings and when he left the room, the officers voted their confidence in Congress and asked the General to act in their behalf.

More sinister was a proposal to Washington made shortly after the fighting ended. Colonel John Lewis Nicola of New York wrote Washington to urge him to overthrow the American republic and make himself king. Nicola claimed there were other Army officers who would support a military coup. Washington angrily rejected such a plot. He was devoted to a democratic republic and would not think of conspiring for dictatorship or a monarchy. He was no Caesar to exploit his military prestige and power to set himself upon a throne.

Soon after, it became apparent that the British had lost heart with the surrender at Yorktown. They had no taste for serious fighting and began to leave their posts and fortresses and sail home. Parliament and the king ordered negotiations to begin at Paris with the American peace envoys, Benjamin Franklin, John Adams, and John Jay. In the Treaty of Paris, signed on September 3, 1783, the Americans won more than they had hoped for. The British acknowledged the independence of the United States, giving it control of all the western lands up to the Mississippi—the lands Britain had won from France in 1763. Spain, which held the great unmapped territory beyond the Mississippi, won back Florida and a strip along the Gulf Coast including New Orleans. France, however, ridden with the intrigue and financial disorder that fore-shadowed its own revolution, got back only the islands in the West Indies captured by the British.

As he waited for news of the signing of the peace treaty, Washington's thoughts turned to retirement. He wanted nothing more than to spend the rest of his days at Mount Vernon, savoring again the joys of a planter's life. He wrote a last message to the states for whose freedom he had fought, suggesting what he believed essential to a happy future for the new nation. He hoped for "an indissoluble Union" of the states under one national government, a government that would exercise "a sacred regard to public justice," and for peace among the nations. Lastly, he asked Americans to forget their local prejudices and sacrifice personal advantage to reach the common agreement that would secure prosperity for all.

After Clinton's last troops had sailed away from New York, Washington said farewell to the officers of his vanishing army in a final meeting at Fraunces Tavern.

Washington's farewell to his officers
at Fraunces Tavern in New York

When they had raised their last glass of wine to one
another, tears came to the general's eyes. "I cannot come
to each of you," he said, his voice shaking, "but shall
feel obliged if each of you will come and take me by the
hand." As he looked the first man in the eye, he put his
arms around him and kissed him on the cheek. With
tears flowing, they all came up to him in turn and received
his embrace. Then the general raised his arm in silent
farewell, and walking out of the tavern, started for home.

Through Philadelphia and Wilmington and Baltimore he rode, greeted by escorts of honor and great celebrations along the way. At Annapolis, standing before the Congress, he resigned his commission, saying, "Having now finished the work assigned me, I retire from the great theatre of action; and bidding an affectionate farewell to this august body under whose orders I have so long acted, I here offer my commission, and take my leave of all the employments of public life."

The next morning—the day before Christmas—George Washington, private citizen, was home again.

CHAPTER NINE
Private Citizen

Washington settled into Mount Vernon, older by eight years than when he had left his home. For a while the life of a private citizen seemed unreal. His time was his own, but there was little to do, for snow and ice kept him housebound. "I am retiring within myself," he wrote cheerfully to Lafayette, "envious of none and determined to be pleased with all."

Certainly all were more than pleased with him. He had become a legend in his own lifetime. He did not have the magnetism of an Alexander the Great, the eloquence of a Jefferson, the genius of a Franklin. Yet he was idolized like a noble Roman of the ancient world. He even looked like one of their portrait busts or statues. His quiet faith, when so many others doubted and hesitated, made his countrymen believe with him that the new America would succeed and prosper. His honor was their honor. His sense of duty became theirs. His integrity was the standard for all. The longer he led the Revolution, the less he seemed an individual, and the more he became a symbol. It was an outcome he did not desire or foresee.

What had often seemed to be a hopeless revolt had been successful in part because of the persistence of Washington. The Americans lost many of the battles, but they won the crucial victory, the last battle. Military historians do not count Washington among the great chiefs. He was no Napoleon. Yet he was a fighter who never lost sight of the final goal. Against the greatest odds, he was able to raise and train and direct an army that defeated the best Europe had.

From the revolt of the American colonies the world outside learned a lesson. In years to come other colonies of the British Empire (Canada was the first of many) would govern themselves with little or no control from London. It was an unprecedented development in the history of empires. Like Britain, many great powers found how hard it is to put down a popular rising in a country when its people have pride in themselves and the desire to be free.

Washington took advantage of the first winter weeks at home to catch up on his reading of history. After years in the saddle a quiet time by the fireside was welcome. When the bad weather lifted he found dozens of neglected duties to attend to—accounts needing to be straightened, rents to be collected, a terrace to be paved, a greenhouse to be built, slaves to be looked after.

Eighteen of Washington's slaves had run away during a British raid on his district. Nine others had been sold in his absence to provide money for taxes. The Revolution had done little to change their condition. When the Declaration of Independence said that "all men are created equal," Blacks wondered, how can any person be a slave if that is true? Slavery troubled white men who led the Revolution for freedom, and yet were slaveholders. Thinking of slavery, Thomas Jefferson said, "I tremble for my country when I reflect that God is just, that his justice cannot sleep forever." Patrick Henry declared, "I will not, I cannot justify it." And Washington wrote, "I shall be happily mistaken if they [the slaves] are not found to be a very troublesome species of property ere many years have passed over our heads."

The founding fathers interpreted that phrase, "created equal," in a limited way. The common people took the phrase more literally. Throughout the Revolution Blacks called for the end of slavery, reminding the whites how strange it was to shout "Liberty or Death!" while holding three-quarters of a million black Americans in bondage.

Yet Blacks fought in the American struggle for independence from the beginning. About 5,000 of them, both slave and free, served under Washington's command, most of them in mixed units with whites, and in both the North and the South. Only two colonies, Georgia and South Carolina, refused to enlist black soldiers. They paid for their racism, for each lost about 25,000 slaves who ran off to the British upon the promise of freedom, a promise often broken.

When Washington rode off to war he took with him an old servant named Peter, and the young slave William Lee. Lee went through the terrible winter at Valley Forge with him, and was at the siege of Yorktown. When the war was over and liberty won, many of the black soldiers found the promise of freedom made by slaveholders was not always fulfilled. The Virginia legislature in 1783 passed a law freeing all slaves who had "contributed toward the establishment of American Liberty and Independence." In spite of the act of emancipation, many masters refused to notify their slaves. Even William Lee was not set free until the death of Washington.

Lafayette, his intimate friend, asked Washington to join him in a plan to emancipate slaves and establish a colony for them where they would become tenants on the land and earn their own way. Washington replied, "I shall be happy to join you in so laudable a work." But he never did. Lafayette became disillusioned with America as the Cradle of Liberty. From France he wrote, "I would never have drawn my sword in the cause of America if I could have conceived that thereby I was founding a land of slavery."

Although Washington's plantation was comparatively free of brutality, the Blacks were not resigned to slavery. Some of his slaves ran away, as we have seen. Freedom, however risky, was better than a master, however benevolent. He disapproved of abolitionist attempts to liberate slaves. In 1786 when Quakers tried to help a neighbor's slave to escape, Washington wrote a friend: "I can only say that there is not a man living who wishes more sincerely than I do, to see a plan adopted for the abolition of it [slavery]; but there is only one proper and effectual mode by which it can be accomplished, and that is by Legislative authority; and this, as far as my suffrage will go, shall never be wanting."

But "conspiracies" to free slaves he had no use for. A few months after this letter, he lost a slave of his own, who escaped from "the care of a trusty overseer." Ten

*A portrait of George and Martha Washington said to have
been painted by Edward Savage around 1793, with their
adopted children and the President's personal slave, Billy Lee.*

years later a public outcry in Portsmouth, New Hampshire prevented the return of another of Washington's
runaway slaves. He did not push the case, he said, lest
it cause "uneasy sensations in the minds of well-disposed
citizens."

Fame can be a great nuisance. Visitors flocked to Mount Vernon. They stayed as long as they liked; some returned all too often. Wherever he travelled, his pleasure was lessened by the ceremonies and speeches he had to endure. His household was enlarged by a niece, a nephew, and two of Martha's grandchildren. Besides their own half-dozen, the family often had another ten to fifteen guests, invited or not, at meals. Most were welcome, some were distinguished, a few were pests. In any case, they consumed a huge amount of food and drink, which placed a financial burden on Washington. As a national hero, *the* national hero, he had mountains of mail to sift through and answer.

It must have been a relief to journey across the mountains to see what was happening to his western lands. He had heard of squatters on his property and of thieves who were trying to sell tracts that belonged to him. He hoped to revive the old project of linking the upper Ohio with the Virginia rivers. If he could locate a good route for such a road perhaps the states or Congress would finance it.

With his physician and friend, Dr. James Craik, he set out on September 1, 1784. They returned about a month later, after covering 680 miles on horseback. His observations led him to propose that Virginia and Maryland, together with the Congress, make engineering surveys of the public improvements he suggested. He was named president of a Potomac Company to develop waterways and improve Virginia roads.

Washington had come home from the war almost penniless. There were constant demands on him now for money—to improve his plantation, to meet running expenses, to lend family and friends what they asked of him. During these difficult years he was supporting twenty-two nieces and nephews. Many debts others owed him went unpaid. Sometimes he had to refuse promising offers of investment because he didn't have the necessary funds. Yet he never stinted on wining and dining his guests with the best of everything. They would have been shocked to know that at the end of 1785 he had almost no cash on hand.

Twice artists visited to make his portrait. The first was Robert Pine, an English painter whose support of the Revolution had cost him his livelihood. When a mutual friend wrote urging Washington to see Pine, he agreed in this amusing fashion:

> In for a penny, in for a pound is an old adage. I am so hackneyed to the touches of the painters' pencil that I am now altogether at their beck, and sit like patience on a monument while they are delineating the lines of my face. It is a proof among many others of what habit and custom can effect. At first I was as impatient at the request, and as restive under the operation as a colt is of the saddle. The next time I submitted very reluctantly, but with less flouncing. Now, no dray moves more readily to the thill than I to the painter's chair. It may easily be conceived therefore that I yielded a ready obedience to your request and to the views of Mr. Pine.

The French sculptor, Jean Antoine Houdon, was next. The Virginia legislature had ordered a statue of Wash-

A plaster bust of Washington made from the
original life cast by Houdon, done at Mount
Vernon in October, 1785. The French sculptor
cast it from a life mask, and it is perhaps the
closest likeness we have to the real man.

ington, and Thomas Jefferson, then in France, commissioned Houdon to do it. The sculptor crossed the Atlantic with three assistants and an interpreter. They were put up at Mount Vernon for the two weeks it took to model the statue.

In time Washington sought relief from the unending demands of visitors. Surely he took pride in his house and lands and table and the fine impression they made on his guests. But he withdrew into a routine. Breakfast was at seven, and the morning was set aside for work. Dinner was at two in the afternoon, and then he left his guests for at least two hours. Sometimes he did not come down to the evening's supper. Nine was his usual bedtime.

At the end of 1786 he took on a private secretary, Tobias Lear. Only twenty-four, Lear was a New Hampshire man and a Harvard graduate who had lived a while in Europe and handled French well. He was an affable and hard-working man who became a warm companion to Washington, almost a son, and stayed with him until the general's death.

Washington decided he could do more with his plantation and took over its management himself. He made his young nephew, George A. Washington, his assistant. He hired a highly recommended practical English farmer to help introduce new methods. Leasing more land, he revived his youthful skill at surveying and laid out six farms. Almost daily he rode the rounds of them all, some twenty miles, recording whatever was being done and the effect it had. An overseer ran each farm, using the labor of the 200 or more slaves owned by Washington and Martha. The new methods were intended to yield food or marketable crops without exhausting the soil. While not perfect, the results were a marked improvement. He continued to do business too at his mill and his fishery.

Little that he tried made money, for in the mid-1780s a depression struck both Europe and America. Bad times were made worse because there was no stable national currency or good credit sources. The planters like Washington were hardest hit and so too were small farmers unable to meet debts to merchants or payments on mortages.

Washington's health weakened in these years of retirement. A chronic fever bedded him and rheumatic pains dogged him in the winter. He didn't complain. Wasn't he in his fifties now, and "descending the hill?" What could one expect of a man who came from so "short-lived a family?" He heard often of the death of his old comrades, sometimes finding it too painful to express his sorrow in words. When General Nathaniel Greene died, leaving his business affairs in a mess, Washington wrote Mrs. Greene that he hoped she would let him pay the expenses of giving her son (named after him) the best education possible, in whatever field the boy chose.

That year Washington's younger brothers, Samuel and John, died too. Then his niece Frances Bassett, who had married his secretary Tobias Lear, lost her first baby. Bad political news intruded on his grief. Civil war had broken out in western Massachusetts. The poor farmers and villagers were up in arms. Ragged and penniless at the end of the Revolutionary War, they had headed home without the pay long overdue them. Congress, itself without funds, had asked the states to pay the wages owed the soldiers. But many of the states failed to act.

Back home, the ex-soldiers found themselves deeply in debt, mainly to Boston merchants. They feared the courts would foreclose on their farms. A war veteran, Captain Daniel Shays, organized 1,500 men to descend with pitchforks on the courts and prevent them from sitting. They broke into jails and freed prisoners held for debt. The frightened judges promised not to act until the farmers' grievances had been settled.

Shays' Rebellion terrified many of the Revolution's leaders. Conservatives in Europe and America had always predicted that a government of the people could only end in anarchy. If Shays' Rebellion spread, what power could put it down? The Congress could not muster an army against it because it still had no funds to pay soldiers.

Washington was appalled by the news from the north. He never expected to see "such a formidable rebellion against the laws and constitutions of our own making." The immediate danger passed when the governor of Massachusetts sent 4,000 state troops out to prevent Shays' attack upon the U.S. arsenal at Springfield. The rebels were defeated—and four of them were killed—in a brief skirmish on January 26, 1787.

The uprising revealed how helpless the weak government was in an emergency. From 1781 the states had governed themselves in a loose alliance under the Articles of Confederation. These articles gave little power to the national Congress. It could not raise revenues, it could not regulate commerce between the states, laws could not be passed without agreement of three-fourths of the thirteen states. And even when laws were enacted,

CANADA

St. Lawrence River

Lake Superior

Lake Michigan

Lake Huron

Lake Erie

Lake Ontario

NORTHWEST

TERRITORY

CLAIMED BY N.Y.

N.H.

NEW YORK

MASSACHUSETTS

CLAIMED BY MASS. AND N.Y.

CONN.

RHODE ISLAND

PENNSYLVANIA

NEW JERSEY

MD.

DEL.

VIRGINIA

CLAIMED BY VA.

CLAIMED BY N.C.

NORTH CAROLINA

CLAIMED BY S.C.

SOUTH CAROLINA

CLAIMED BY GA.

MISSISSIPPI TERRITORY

GEORGIA

CLAIMED BY U.S. GA. & SPAIN

SPANISH FLORIDA

ATLANTIC OCEAN

GULF OF MEXICO

- - - Boundary of 1783

Original thirteen states

Territory from Great Britain, 1783

Spanish territory

THE UNITED STATES, 1787

the national Congress had no power to enforce them. To the world, this American effort at self-government looked pitiful. Only a few months before Shays' Rebellion, Virginia and a few other states had called for a national convention to meet in Philadelphia to strengthen the constitution of the federal government so that it could better meet the needs of the Union. Shays' Rebellion helped to muster support for the convention.

Knowing that Washington's influence would be a great asset, Virginia asked him to head its delegation to the Constitutional Convention. It will interrupt your private life only briefly, they told him. But he knew better. He would be the most prominent man there, except for Benjamin Franklin, who in his eighties was too old to take leadership. If the convention failed, Washington's reputation would be badly injured. If it succeeded, he would be expected to do all in his power to launch the strengthened government on its new course.

He was torn by conflicting feelings. Should he stay at home and keep the promise of withdrawal from public life he had made to the country, to himself, to Martha? Or go to Philadelphia and perhaps be accused of gross personal ambition? But if he failed to go, what if the convention foundered on conflicts of interest for lack of the strong leadership he might give it?

In the end he agreed to go.

CHAPTER TEN

Making a Constitution

Washington set out in his carriage for Philadelphia early in May 1787. He was welcomed warmly by affectionate citizens who knew he had given up his precious retirement to serve them once more. As he waited for the delegates to arrive, he met daily with other Virginians to discuss a plan for a new national government that Madison and Randolph had developed. The convention opened in the red brick State House on May 25; all voted for Washington to be President of the convention. He took the chair, wearing his splendid suit of black, and for sixteen exhausting weeks during that hot summer presided over the intense debate. He listened most of the time, stepping down from the chair now and then to cast a vote.

These fifty-five delegates talking together in Philadelphia were not idealists dreaming of a utopian government. They were men experienced in the world's ways—lawyers, soldiers, governors, planters, legislators, businessmen, merchants, inventors. They had seen human nature in action in courtrooms, marketplaces, legislatures, battlefields. They had themselves contended for power and wealth. They knew human passions can be boundless and violent. They had lived under a royal government which had oppressed them; they learned that power grows when there is no equal power to control it.

They had no illusions about changing the nature of human beings to fit some ideal system. Yet they did believe in democracy. Where but in the people must the ultimate power of government reside? The mass of citizens must make the laws that they are to obey, and choose the officials who are to administer them. Since men act on self-interest by their nature, then government must be strong enough to control any tendency to greed and corruption. But strong government is itself a threat to liberty, so effective limits must be set upon governmental authority.

The delegates had their differences, of course. Washington helped mightily to bridge those differences at the convention. He thought of himself first of all as an American. He had fought for the country, not for any selfish regional or economic advantage. He looked to the national welfare and the common good. But he knew the smaller states envied the larger, the Yankees and the southerners distrusted one another, commercial interests opposed agricultural interests, the rich and the poor felt threatened by each other. Even as he had left the army for private life Washington had publicly appealed to all Americans to find the way to make themselves free and happy on this "vast tract of continent abounding with all the necessaries and conveniences of life."

Now the fifty-five delegates set themselves to that task. They came from twelve of the thirteen states. (Only

W E the People of the States of New-Hampſhire, Maſſachuſetts, Rhode-Iſland and Providence Plan-tations, Connecticut, New-York, New-Jerſey, Penn-ſylvania, Delaware, Maryland, Virginia, North-Caro-lina, South-Carolina, and Georgia, do ordain, declare and eſtabliſh the following Conſtitution for the Govern-ment of Ourſelves and our Poſterity.

ARTICLE I.
The ſtile of this Government ſhall be, " The United States of America."

II.
The Government ſhall conſiſt of ſupreme legiſlative, executive and judicial powers.

III.
The legiſlative power ſhall be veſted in a Congreſs, to conſiſt of two ſeparate and diſtinct bodies of men, a Houſe of Repreſentatives, and a Senate ; ~~each of which ſhall, in all caſes, have a negative on the other. The Legiſlature ſhall meet on the firſt Monday in December in every year.~~

*The legiſlature ſhall meet at least once in every year and that meeting ſhall be on the firſt Monday in December unleſs a different day ſhall be appointed by law.

IV.
Sect. 1. The Members of the Houſe of Repreſentatives ſhall be choſen eve-ry ſecond year, by the people of the ſeveral States comprehended within this Union. The qualifications of the electors ſhall be the ſame, from time to time, as thoſe of the electors in the ſeveral States, of the moſt numerous branch of their own legiſlatures.

Sect. 2. Every Member of the Houſe of Repreſentatives ſhall be of the age of twenty-five years at leaſt ; ſhall have been a citizen in the United States for at leaſt ~~three~~ years before his election ; and ſhall be, at the time of his e-lection, ~~a reſident~~ of the State in which he ſhall be choſen.

Sect. 3. The Houſe of Repreſentatives ſhall, at its firſt formation, and until the number of citizens and inhabitants ſhall be taken in the manner herein af-ter deſcribed, conſiſt of ſixty-five Members, of whom three ſhall be choſen in New-Hampſhire, eight in Maſſachuſetts, one in Rhode-Iſland and Providence Plantations, five in Connecticut, ſix in New-York, four in New-Jerſey. eight in Pennſylvania, one in Delaware, ſix in Maryland, ten in Virginia, five in North-Carolina, five in South-Carolina, and three in Georgia.

Sect. 4. As the proportions of numbers in the different States will alter from time to time ; as ſome of the States may hereafter be divided ; as others may be enlarged by addition of territory ; as two or more States may be united ; as new States will be erected within the limits of the United States, the Legiſla-ture ſhall, in each of theſe caſes, regulate the number of repreſentatives by the number of inhabitants, according to the ~~~~ the rate of one for every forty thouſand. *Provided that every State ſhall have at leaſt one repreſentative.*

Sect. 5. All bills for raiſing or appropriating money, and for fixing the ſala-ries of the officers of government, ſhall originate in the Houſe of Repreſenta-tives, and ſhall not be altered or amended by the Senate. No money ſhall be drawn from the public Treaſury, but in purſuance of appropriations that ſhall originate in the Houſe of Repreſentatives.

Sect. 6. The Houſe of Repreſentatives ſhall have the ſole power of impeach-ment. It ſhall chooſe its Speaker and other officers.

Sect. 7. Vacancies in the Houſe of Repreſentatives ſhall be ſupplied by writs of election from the executive authority of the State, in the repreſentation from which they ſhall happen.   V.

While Washington presided over the Constitutional Convention in Philadelphia, he made notes on the various drafts. Here are his corrections on a first page.

one, Rhode Island, was absent.) Most of the men agreed that thorough political change was needed. They worked behind closed doors—better to argue out their differences quietly and then submit their conclusions to the nation. A Virginia Plan for a new constitution was put up for debate first. The arguments dragged on. Sometimes it seemed nothing would get done. By July, Washington wrote a friend he almost despaired of a favorable outcome. For many hours each day he presided, growing tired and bored, fearing it might all collapse. For relief there was a steady round of dinners, a visit to his old camp at Valley Forge, riding into the country, fishing in the Schuylkill.

Gradually the delegates worked their way to resolution of their differences. Compromise of course was the path they had to take if they were to achieve anything meaningful and lasting. A major issue was the division of power—between the central government and the states, and between the larger and smaller states. Another was the conflict between the agricultural South and the commercial North. The convention could have split apart on these questions if the delegates had not chosen to "hang together" rather than separately.

The deadlock between the bigger and smaller states was broken by giving something to both. There would be two chambers in the Congress. In the lower, the House of Representatives, representation would be on the basis of population, pleasing the larger states. In the upper house, the Senate, the smaller states got equal representation—two members elected from each state.

The differences between North and South were reconciled by two major compromises. One granted Congress the right to regulate trade, which the commercial

North, with large investments in shipping, desired. And it forbade Congress to enact duties on exports, which the agricultural South depended on for its income.

The second compromise dealt with slavery, the dominant issue between the two regions. The delegates permitted slavery to remain legal to keep the lower South, where it was important for the production of major crops, in the Union. An agreement was reached that allowed the South to count three-fifths of its slaves as a basis for representation in Congress. The African slave trade was allowed to go on for another twenty years. And the states were required to return fugitive slaves to their owners.

These were great gains for the slaveholders. But they paid a price for it. While the Convention adopted these clauses, the Congress, meeting in New York, enacted the Northwest Ordinance. It prohibited slavery north of the Ohio River. (Later, as North and South tried to extend their power through new states to be formed in the West, they would come to a bloody showdown over slavery.)

Now the Convention moved to less quarrelsome issues. With the nature of the legislative branch decided, everyone agreed there must also be an executive branch of government and a judiciary. But how to choose them? Finally the delegates determined that a president would be chosen by a majority of electors authorized to vote by each of the states. If the electors failed to make a choice, Congress would have that power. The president would head the executive branch, with a veto over acts of Congress that only a two-thirds majority of both houses could override. He would manage foreign affairs, direct the armed forces, and make federal appointments subject to Congressional approval. There would be an independent federal judiciary with judges appointed for life. A Supreme Court would be the highest court of appeal.

A system of separation of powers was agreed upon. It meant the legislative, executive, and judicial arms of government would have different powers. The Congress would pass the laws, the president would see they were carried out, and the Supreme Court would resolve disputes. The aim was to prevent concentration of power in any branch, thus frustrating the growth of tyranny.

But suppose any of these branches did try to destroy the others? Against that possibility the Convention guaranteed each of them the power to check the other's actions. The president could veto the laws of Congress. The Senate could disapprove the president's treaties and refuse office to people he selected. The president could appoint judges, but those judges could declare unlawful certain acts of the president and his assistants. Congress would have certain powers, but the judges could decide when Congress went beyond its proper authority.

Majority rule was a fundamental principle the delegates wanted the Constitution to guarantee. The Congress would be elected by majority vote, and would pass laws only when a majority agreed. Elections would be held often so that the people could vote on whether they liked or disliked what the candidates stood for or did.

Rule by majority can be mean and oppressive if a minority is disliked or despised. So the Constitution must ensure that a minority's rights can't be violated or ignored just because a majority wants to. The Constitution would guarantee certain unalienable rights to all, no matter what their color, faith, language, or point of view. To shield judges from pressure, they would hold office for life. Then they need not fear a majority's anger when they protected the rights of an unpopular minority.

The delegates did not want the hand of the dead to bind the living. They knew they were not perfect nor could the Constitution be perfect. Making mistakes was human; correcting them should be made possible. They foresaw that the nation would grow and social needs would change. So the Constitution must be open to alteration. An amendment procedure was spelled out and it has been used many times to modify the Constitution. Both acts of Congress and rulings of the Supreme Court have elaborated the basic document in the 200 years since its adoption.

On September 17 the delegates met for the last time. They went over a printed text of the Constitution containing all the revisions agreed upon. At 6:00 P.M., with Washington in the chair, the roll was called on the motion to agree to the document as amended. The majority in every state voted "Aye." The delegates signed the Constitution and walked over to the City Tavern for a farewell dinner together.

(How do we know what happened in the secret sessions at Philadelphia? The drafts of proposals, the debates over them, the agreements worked out? James Madison, one of the Virginia delegates, kept a verbatim record. It was not made public until over fifty years later, in 1840.)

What they had set out to do and completed is best expressed in the Preamble to the Constitution:

The signing of the Constitution at Philadelphia on September 17, 1787

We the People of the United States, in order to form a more perfect Union, establish Justice, insure domestic Tranquility, provide for the common defense, promote the general Welfare, and secure the Blessings of Liberty to ourselves and our Posterity, do ordain and establish this Constitution for the United States of America.

Students of the Constitution agree that it is "one of the world's masterpieces of practical statecraft." As Washington rode home, he thought back on the months of debate, carried on at an intellectual level so rare in politics. How many conflicts had to be conciliated, local prejudices overcome, sacrifices made for the general welfare. It had made the task so difficult and intricate, he wrote to a friend, that "I think it is much to be wondered at, that anything could have been produced with such unanimity." It was his very presence in Philadelphia that helped give the uncertain experiment the dignity and credibility it needed. He was the key figure of the Constitutional Convention.

Philadelphia gave the world a superb demonstration of the art of democratic politics. Out of the collective experience of enormously talented professional politicians came a Constitution that established a new and far better national government. It would be stable, and yet allow for change. Only 4,000 words long, it is the world's oldest written living constitution. It set an example for nation-building that many countries—freed from colonial rule, from authoritarian regimes or totalitarian dictatorships—would learn from.

This chapter of history, wrote the historian Henry Steele Commager,

> was assuredly the most creative in the history of politics. How sobering to recall that every major political institution we now possess was invented before the year 1800 and that not one has been created since. Making a nation was new (none had been deliberately created before); popular self-government was new; successful federalism, separation of powers, judicial independence and judicial review were new. The "exact subordination" of the military to the civil power was new,

and so too that most revolutionary of all experiments—the separation of church and state.

Reaching Mount Vernon on September 22, Washington slipped again into the daily life of a planter. He had been gone "four months and 14 days," he noted in his journal. There was much to catch up on at his farms. He had to scurry about for cash to pay his taxes and debts. But most of all he must do everything possible to have the new Constitution ratified.

It would not be easy. State conventions elected specially for this purpose would vote on the Constitution. When nine of the states had approved the Constitution, it would go into effect for those states. There was noisy opposition to the Constitution. Since most of the delegates had been upper-class, how could they speak for the people? Wouldn't federal rule be as overbearing as that of George III? And where was the Bill of Rights? The Constitution's most ardent supporters were needed to help swing the reluctant behind the new plan. Washington thought the life of the country hung by a thread. If the Constitution were not endorsed, government would collapse.

But it was impossible for him to campaign publicly for the Constitution. Everyone believed he would become the first president under the new system, should it come into being. He himself knew he would be nominated. He did not want anyone to say he was working for his own elevation to the highest office in the land. Best to support the Constitution privately then, urging those who agreed with him to get out and campaign for its adoption, and inducing others at least to soften their opposition. He wrote to Lafayette that ratification "will determine the political fate of America for the present generation and probably produce no small influence on the happiness of society through a long succession of ages to come." In the public debate over adoption many pamphlets appeared arguing one side or the other. A series of essays called the Federalist papers was written by Hamilton, Madison, and John Jay. The essays helped place Washington and others firmly behind the Constitution.

Many arguments were marshalled against the Constitution. To all of them its champions made answer. One of the most effective defenses was the personal one. The great Benjamin Franklin had endorsed the Constitution. And the nation's hero, George Washington, had presided over its making. Since it was certain that he would become the first president, that was proof against all danger of tyranny. He had refused to use the army to seize power. He would always stand up for freedom. Even the radicals had to face the facts. Government in both the states and Congress in the years since the Revolution had been chaotic and unreliable. The wiser ones now saw that a swing toward greater order had to come.

Delaware was the first state to ratify, by unanimous vote, in December 1787. One after another the states came in, but often after a strong contest with the outcome in doubt till the last ballot. A switch of two, three, ten votes in some important states would have defeated the Constitution. Only the promise of a Bill of Rights finally settled the outcome. By June 21, 1788, nine states had ratified. The Constitution was now in effect.

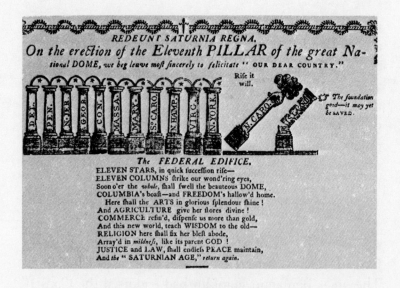

A newspaper, the Massachusetts Sentinel, *employed cartoon and verse to urge the two remaining holdouts—North Carolina and Rhode Island—to ratify the Constitution. All thirteen states approved it by the end of May 1790.*

It marked a special moment in American history—the end of revolutionary upheaval and the beginning of citizenship in a democracy. The new republic would endure. Americans were now more than cogs in an imperial machine. The world had truly been turned upside down. Power had been shifted from the monarch to his subjects. In ratifying the Constitution, the ruled had become the rulers. They hailed their future with processions, dinners, fireworks, celebrations of every kind.

In a few months they would elect a Congress and a president.

CHAPTER ELEVEN

Mr. President

*I*f the new government was to succeed, no one but George Washington must preside at its launching. Everyone wanted it. On February 4, 1789, he was unanimously elected President of the United States, with John Adams as his Vice President. He set out from Mount Vernon in April, coaching over the rutted roads to New York, the first capital of the nation. I am "entering upon an unexplored field," he said, "enveloped on every side with clouds and darkness." He felt like a condemned man going to the place of execution. After a long life taken up with public cares why must he quit his peaceful farm to plunge into an ocean of troubles?

To the huge crowds that met him on the eight-day journey he was "our adored leader and ruler." They said it with banners, parades, speeches, editorials. Yet the tributes only filled him with anxiety. He had accepted the nomination when convinced it was for the good of the country. But he doubted he had the political skill to steer the government safely. He told himself he would leave office as soon as his services were no longer needed.

Washington greeted by the people of New York
as he arrives by boat from New Jersey to take
office in the temporary capital in April 1789

On April 30 he was inaugurated president at Federal
Hall. For the occasion he wore a suit of brown broadcloth
made in Massachusetts, with silk stockings, silver shoe-
buckles, and a dress sword. A joint committee of Congress escorted him in a grand coach drawn by four fine
horses and flanked by a military procession. When it was
time to take the oath of office he stepped out on the
balcony of Federal Hall overlooking Wall and Broad

Streets. The streets, the windows, the rooftops were crowded with cheering citizens. Washington put his right hand on the Bible as Chancellor Robert Livingston of New York administered the oath:

"Do you solemnly swear that you will faithfully execute the office of President of the United States and will, to the best of your ability, preserve, protect, and defend the Constitution of the United States?"

"I solemnly swear," Washington answered, and repeated the oath, adding, "So help me God." He bent and kissed the Bible. Livingston turned to the crowd and shouted, "Long live the President of the United States!" Joyously the people roared back, "God bless our President!" Washington bowed, to more cheers, then went inside to the Senate Chamber to give his inaugural address.

He spoke in a grave, sometimes trembling voice. He thanked Providence for helping the American people to find liberty and happiness under a government made by themselves, and urged a spirit of compromise in the pursuit of decisions affecting the public welfare. His simple, brief speech moved the audience to tears.

That night the streets of New York were packed with people celebrating the birth of their new nation. Scores of taverns rang with music and laughter. Washington was left alone, to dine privately in the presidential home at 3 Cherry Street. Heaven knew how uncertain and difficult his course would be. Harder, he thought, than the command of the Revolutionary Army he had accepted in 1775. That struggle had changed American history. What he must do now could change world history. The new government was an experiment in de-

mocracy. It could prove to the world that Americans—
or any people—could govern themselves. If America failed,
liberty might die and with it the hopes of humankind
everywhere. Was he equal to the responsibility? If he was
not, his guilt would be too much to bear.

Washington started with little of use from the Confederation government. He was left with a dozen clerks,
an army of 672 officers and men, and heavy debts. With
Congress he had to find means to raise money, to build
a national defense, to deal with the Indians. The new
republic had to organize territories, establish federal courts,
regulate trade. A bag of loose and ragged diplomatic
problems was dumped on him by the Confederation. To
fill executive, judicial, and diplomatic posts the president
had to make hundreds of individual choices from the
thousands of men who clamored for well-paying jobs.

Luckily a peaceful and prosperous summer seemed
ahead. It was spoiled by a deep tumor in Washington's
thigh that threatened his life. Extensive surgery was done—
this at a time before anesthetics could ease the pain. The
operation was successful, but it took six weeks for him
to recover his strength. Then his mother, at 81, died of
cancer of the breast. He had never felt close to her. All
through the Revolution he had not written to her once.
Still, her passing reminded him of how short his years
might be.

Back at his desk, Washington had only his old Mount
Vernon aide, Tobias Lear, to help him. In the next
months he took on four more men as assistants. On the
executive level he began only with Vice-President John
Adams. The Massachusetts leader had differed with

Washington on many issues. Their mutual coolness prevented a close working relationship. Adams remained in the background, where most presidents in future would keep their vice-president.

No cabinet was provided for in the Constitution. What Washington and the first Congress did in the next months about this and many other matters set precedents for the future. Congress established the great departments of executive government, and the president appointed the officers to head them. For secretary of the treasury, the most vital post at the time, he appointed his brilliant friend and comrade-in-arms, the young Alexander Hamilton of New York. The equally brilliant Virginian, Thomas Jefferson, became secretary of state. Another Virginian, Edmund Randolph, was made the attorney general. The War Department was entrusted to war veteran Henry Knox of Massachusetts. These four officers made up Washington's cabinet. They began to meet as a group, a custom that has endured. (Congress later added new executive departments as the business of government expanded.) The Congress gave the president the crucial power to remove his executive officers as well as to appoint them.

For chief justice of the Supreme Court, Washington chose John Jay, a New Yorker with considerable experience as lawyer, legislator, and diplomat. There was little for the court to do; it would be years before major cases reached it for decision.

The president's duties were only sketched in the Constitution. His salary was set by Congress at $25,000, a large sum then, and many times greater than the pay

A reception held by the president and the First Lady during his administration in New York, from an engraving by Ritchie, 1861.

of the cabinet and the Congress. What to call the president? The title was debated in private and public; finally common usage let it be simply "Mr. President."

Washington liked to live handsomely, and sometimes had to draw pay in advance to meet his bills. There were fourteen white servants and seven slaves to care for the family, and a coach drawn by six horses. With Martha presiding at table, food and wine were as lavishly served as in Virginia. To hold open house here was impossible, however, so Washington held Tuesday receptions open to any man without invitation, while Martha had tea parties weekly for men and women. Official dinners came on Thursdays. The Washingtons refused private invitations, but went out with guests to enjoy the theater. The country began to celebrate the president's birthday annually, as though he were a king. It was hard for so shy a man to avoid feeling self-important under such constant attention. Perhaps Martha, always modest and simple, helped George to keep his head.

That first year Washington, as chief executive officer, saw to it that measures adopted by Congress were put into effect. His attitude toward the House and Senate was to stand somewhat apart. Both he and the Congress took care to respect the separation of powers. They were self-conscious about what precedents they might set. The first Congress went well. It imposed import duties to bring in considerable revenue. That money helped finance the federal machinery and establish the nation's credit.

High on the agenda was a Bill of Rights. Congress recognized the force of public demand for specific guarantees in the Constitution of personal rights and liberties. In the form of the first ten amendments, the Bill of Rights went through without much trouble. The amendments provided, among other things, that Congress must not abridge freedom of religion, or of the press, or of speech, or of assembly; that the people are "to be secure in their person, houses, papers and effects, against unreasonable search and seizures;" that the right of trial by an impartial jury shall be preserved in both civil and criminal cases; and finally, that all powers not specifically delegated to the United States government are reserved to the states or to the people.

Originally the first ten amendments prohibited only the federal government from interfering with basic rights of citizens. Not until after the Civil War did the 14th Amendment make the Bill of Rights apply to the states also.

The many offices in the new departments of government had to be filled as soon as possible. Appointments plagued Washington as they would all his successors. The party system had not yet risen; he did not have to weigh political loyalty against ability. Nor would he favor family. He appointed the best and most experienced men he could find. If candidates had served well in the Revolution, and were otherwise well-qualified, his heart inclined toward them.

The key appointments he made were Hamilton and Jefferson. They dominated the cabinet and had the greatest influence on Washington's decisions. The remarkable Jefferson, eleven years younger than Washington, was a Renaissance man—lawyer, diplomat, scholar, architect, inventor, writer, philosopher, politician. He lacked only military experience. Born rich and married rich, he owned even more land than Washington. He enjoyed a planter's life on his handsome Monticello estate. Like Washington he was an impressive figure—over six-feet, slim, freckled, red-haired. Washington knew the Virginian well and trusted him. As Minister to France for five years, Jefferson had become familiar with European affairs, and had been witness to the great French Revolution now under way.

The dashing Hamilton, about twenty-three years younger than Washington, had been born in the West

A Currier & Ives lithograph of Washington with his cabinet. From the left: Washington, Secretary of War Henry Knox, Secretary of the Treasury Alexander Hamilton, Secretary of State Thomas Jefferson, and Attorney General Edmund Randolph.

Indies. Left to himself when quite young, he had moved to New York and at twenty had joined Washington's army as an artillery officer and personal aide to the general. In the Revolution he showed great intellectual power, and proved to be brave, honest, and a hard-worker. He was now a lawyer and an expert in financial matters. His marriage into the New York aristocracy placed him among the powerful men of affairs. He came highly recommended for the Treasury post.

The two men were complex studies in personality. Jefferson, champion of the common man, came of upper-class Virginia stock. Hamilton, born on the lowest rung of the social ladder, delighted in the aristocracy and feared "the mob." Jefferson wanted America to remain a rural society free of the dirt of cities and the noise of factories. Hamilton saw an industrial age coming and wanted to prepare America for it.

Now, in the 1790s, a political battle arose over whose government this was to be. Would its policies benefit all the people, or only a certain class? As head of Treasury, Hamilton's economic policies favored the well-to-do conservatives. His first job was to put the country on a sound financial basis. The measures he devised for paying off America's big debts put millions in the pockets of a small group of speculators who had bought up obligations of soldiers, farmers, and small businessmen for as little as five cents on the dollar. The money to pay for this handout would come from taxation upon all the people. This favored the North where most of the speculative buying had occurred. His other measures, too, benefited the moneyed seaboard class while pretty much leaving the agricultural South to shift for itself. He meant to strengthen the country by encouraging the growth of industry (which would be based on the cheap labor of women and children). To put the nation on a stable, paying basis was a sound and worthy goal. But the way Hamilton did it caused an uproar. The arrogant young wizard was deaf to protest. He had "long since learned to hold public opinion as of no value," he said.

The uproar continued and grew louder. It came from two groups: southern planters who didn't like having their agriculture taxed to support northern commerce, and the small farmers of North and South who saw business being helped with generous credit while they got no relief from debt and taxation. The first group believed the rights of the states were threatened by federal tyranny. The second attacked the "ins" generally, by which they meant the Federalists, the name for Hamilton's powerful group.

What brought the two anti-Federalist groups together into one political force was Jefferson's leadership. The people he spoke for resented Hamilton's ambitious efforts to expand credit, create a banking system, and encourage manufacture through the power of the federal government. It smacked of favors to the wealthy paid for by the taxes of the "honest, hard-working part of the community."

The Jeffersonians and Hamiltonians battled as though the enemy were devils. But neither side was made up of devils or of saints. Hamilton designed a program to build a powerful and durable United States, and most of what he asked for, Congress granted. Hindsight indicates this was lucky for the nation. Jefferson's dream of an American Arcadia could never have succeeded in the modern world. Yet Jefferson's suspicion of business, his opposition to monopoly, and to government favors to special interests, created a tradition that has inspired many democratic movements ever since.

Where was Washington in all this? Hamilton and Jefferson had become his close advisors. He admired both men and knew they were valued highly by the Congress. He asked both for counsel and listened carefully to their proposals. He encouraged his department heads to take the initiative and express their views freely. He was neither a Hamilton advocate nor a Jefferson advocate. He took the best he could find in both men. His one concern was to make America succeed and to do it peacefully. He believed both agriculture and business should get federal help when needed. He was open to any ideas that would strengthen America.

It soon became apparent to Washington that his chief lieutenants were at war. By early 1791 the two men clashed openly in front of the president. The issue was whether to establish a national bank under government auspices, as Hamilton proposed. The bill for it passed the Congress but created such a storm that Washington asked both men to give him their written opinions as to whether it would be desirable and constitutional. Hamilton of course argued yes. Jefferson contended just the opposite. Washington decided to sign Hamilton's bill, and soon after approved another Hamilton bill to expand revenues by a tax on distilled liquor, the main source of income for many Western farmers. To Jefferson and his followers it seemed Hamilton had seized the reins of government and that the Federalists were about to corrupt American life. As the conflict intensified, Jefferson's party began to call themselves Republicans.

Each leader created a national newspaper to advance his party's views. The Federalists' was the *Gazette of the United States*, while the Republican voice was the *National Gazette*. The president's two most important cabinet men were now quarreling bitterly in public, using their newspapers like artillery to destroy the hated enemy.

When America was warring with Britain, the people had one goal, to break free and build their own democracy. With independence, it was inevitable that differences would come to the surface. At first there were no political parties with platforms carefully worked out, and election campaigns managed by national or state committees. Parties were even distrusted as bad things that would split the republic. But by now the reality of conflicting interests led people to form parties in one state after another. The concerns of the wealthy, of the artisans, the farmers, the merchants, the planters, were different. What you were, how you made your living, affected how you looked at the world. And each group, alone or in combination with others, began to assert itself.

And why not? Didn't the public arena belong to everyone? To get what they want, people must organize. Under Hamilton and Jefferson, the Federalists and the Republicans began to seek public support for their views and to elect to office candidates who would represent those views.

The struggle between the Federalists and Republicans disturbed Washington. Madison, on the other hand, said "Factions are to liberty what air is to fire." But Washington feared it might weaken the Union. A nation still in its infancy needed great care if it was to survive. America could be magnificent one day, but it must have time to grow, to establish habit and tradition that would carry the people through crises without tearing the nation apart. He had the respect and affection of both Hamilton and Jefferson, and he tried to heal the breach between them. An appeal to their loyalty to the nation did no good, for in their minds their differences were too great to be put aside.

As his first term came to its close, Washington wished

fervently to retire from office. The presidency had brought him no joy, only heavy cares. His health was declining; after the tumor early in his term, there was a bout of pneumonia, and now worry about a failing memory. He longed for Mount Vernon. His letters home contained detailed instructions to his overseers, and when Congress was not in session, he hurried south to the plantation.

But could he leave the presidency? Was it the right time?

CHAPTER TWELVE

Farewell

Washington had both domestic and foreign troubles on his mind as he considered whether to serve a second term. The United States faced difficult problems first of all with the Indians on the western borders. Several states had made dubious deals for land with tribal chiefs. It enraged the Indians to see their valuable hunting grounds disappear. When white settlers came in, the Indians attacked them. With their superior manpower and their skill in forest warfare they were a serious military threat.

To meet the danger, Washington got Congress to enlarge the tiny army by one regiment. In 1791, 1,400 soldiers advanced on the Indians in what is now Indiana, only to be ambushed and suffer a terrible defeat. But a year later General Anthony Wayne, with a larger force, won a decisive victory over the Indians in the Ohio region. It made the northwest frontier more secure.

Washington did not think constant fighting was the best solution to relations with the Indians. He tried to get Congress and the states to treat the Indians fairly. Indians should get equal protection under the law and in the courts, he insisted. He proposed that old treaties be re-examined and if any proved to be unjust, the Indians should be given back their land or be paid fairly for it. Jefferson called the idea unconstitutional and insisted on military action, not negotiations.

Washington then came up with another idea. Why not induce the Indians to give up their hunting economy, and adopt farming and handicrafts as a different way of life? Then they would not need huge forests for hunting and could live peaceably in smaller fertile tracts alongside white settlements. It was an impractical proposal that ran counter to what both the Indians and the frontiersmen wanted. Why should the Indians abandon their ancient and treasured cultures. And the whites, tainted by racism and driven by greed, had no desire to live with people they considered savages.

When this idea proved unworkable, Washington did not conceal the truth from the people. He knew honesty won their trust and confidence, and he tried to find out what people thought of their government. Early in his first term he took a month's trip by coach through New England. In his diary he set down impressions of the new factories he visited along the way, of the ships and their cargoes sailing from the ports, of how the farms and villages and roads and taverns looked, and what people were saying. The parades, dinners, poems, and speeches that greeted him sometimes got in the way of his mission. Still, it encouraged him "to see with his own eyes the situation of the country and to learn more accurately the disposition of the people."

Later he toured the southern states, riding down the seaboard to Georgia and back up on the inland route.

The prosperity he had seen in New England was missing down there. Gone for two months this time, Washington travelled only with his coachman and a few servants— no secret service men or guards. He found the people generally pleased with their government, though there were rumors of frontier anger against the whiskey tax. He had an eye for more than political and economic facts. His diary notes the large numbers of attractive women he saw in various places. Again, there were receptions, breakfasts, dinners, speeches, fireworks. The journey showed him he was as popular in the South as in New England.

In the fall of 1790 Washington and the government moved from New York to Philadelphia. It would be the temporary seat of power. The question of a permanent location for the capital had been argued between North and South for a long time. Northerners favored New York or Philadelphia; Southerners wanted a site on the Potomac. A political deal settled the issue. In the debate over Hamilton's economic program, the Treasury chief had induced Jefferson to line up Southern votes for one of his proposals in return for Northern votes to place the capital in the South. It was agreed that the government would sit in Philadelphia for ten years, when the new "Federal City" ought to be ready.

The decision pleased Washington, who was asked by Congress to pick the exact site along the 67-mile stretch of the Potomac. He chose a place only a few miles from Mount Vernon, and put a French engineer, Pierre L'Enfant, in charge of planning the town. L'Enfant looked ahead to the day when the United States would surely be a great nation. He designed a small center for the present, but laid out the land for miles around to preserve the artistic effect during the future growth. With his surveyor's eye Washington followed the planning carefully and took great pleasure in the realization of his vision of a great national city. (Sadly, by the time the new capital—named after him—was built, he was dead. He was the only President never to occupy the White House.)

Now, however, he made his home in the handsome house rented from Robert Morris, a wealthy Philadelphian. Washington had tried, but failed, to find a farm close to the city where he could relax and improve his health. But at least in town he could find the fine food and good company he always enjoyed at Mount Vernon.

And he needed it, for the country's foreign relations were growing more troublesome by the year. In 1789, only a few days after Washington's inauguration, a great revolution had exploded in France. Americans had thrilled at the success of another revolution proclaiming liberty, fraternity, and equality. In its first few years the revolution made sweeping reforms, doing away with the ancient and oppressive privileges of the king, the nobility, and the high clergy. When the royalists and the aristocracy resisted the changes, civil war broke out. The government was taken over by the more radical Jacobins. They got rid of the monarchy and beheaded the king. Not content with rebuilding French society, they began a military crusade to destroy monarchy and privilege throughout Europe.

In the streets of American cities big crowds demonstrated their support of the French revolution. At the news of the king's execution they cheered. The Federalists were alarmed by all the ecstatic marching and cheering. They feared the mob might soon call for American heads of "the wise, the good, the rich" to roll. The Hamilton press denounced the enthusiasts as "filthy Jacobins" and "frog-eating, man-eating cannibals." The crowds only jeered and began to organize Jacobin clubs and call one another "Citizen" in the French manner. Jefferson encouraged them, to Washington's dismay.

In the spring of 1792 the president felt these political quarrels and the daily pressures of office were becoming too much. The second presidential election loomed ahead; he was sixty now and surely someone else could take the leadership. The constant Republican attacks upon the government got under his skin. How long before he himself would be personally insulted?

He told his cabinet he meant to retire to Mount Vernon. They all urged him not to. When he said the rise of party factionalism discouraged him, they said it was all the more reason for him to continue in office. His authority and prestige would fortify the national government. Jefferson argued he was needed to protect the Union from the arrogant Federalists; Hamilton argued he was needed to hold off the bloodthirsty Republicans. Washington tried to make peace between the two men. "Should either of you be so tenacious of your opinions as to make no allowances for those of the other?" he asked. But their antagonism only became sharper. At last he decided he could dampen partisan fires if he held on for another term. No one would oppose him, and both parties pledged to support him.

So again he was elected unanimously, while both parties worked to put their supporters into Congress. In the campaign, partisan spirit ran high, with the press on each side bitterly attacking the opposition. Jefferson's paper even criticized the "monarchical" tone of Washington's weekly receptions and his birthday celebrations.

The sly charge of royal ambition was calculated to ignite Jeffersonian passions as news reached America of crowns threatened by France's military victories in Europe. Crowds huzzahed and cannon roared in celebration. Even when word of the Reign of Terror arrived, with the guillotine slicing off heads endlessly, the American Jacobins were not upset. Had not Jefferson himself said that the tree of liberty must be watered by the blood of tyrants? If it meant desolating half the earth to leave but one Adam and Eve free in every country, he said he was willing to pay the price. He could say that easily, who had never seen men die in bloody anguish as Washington had. The president took no pleasure in the use of organized terror to achieve political goals. He watched as the movement of liberation in France turned into butchery by rival terrorisms. He dreaded men who could murder anyone in the name of the people's good.

In this frame of mind, he reacted badly to the rebellion of farmers in western Pennsylvania against the collection of a federal tax on whiskey. In the summer of 1794 hundreds of them came together in armed resistance and burned the tax collector's offices. In those mountains grain could not be carried across the high ridges in bushel form so it was converted to the liquid form of easily transportable whiskey. Used for barter, it was the only source of income for the farmers. But the tax Hamilton imposed was so heavy it took about 50 percent of the farmer's income—and Hamilton insisted it be paid in

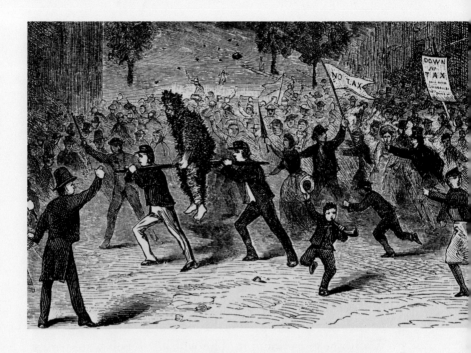

A tax collector is tarred and feathered by
Pennsylvania farmers rebelling in 1794 against the
heavy tax on whiskey, their major source of income.

U.S. currency, which was just what the farmers did not
have. If an equal burden had been placed on every American, it would have brought about the defeat or hanging
of the congressmen who supported it. The Whiskey Rebellion, however, mustered no popular support outside
the isolated region.

At the news of the uprising, Washington lost his
composure. He was furious with "this insurrection" and
called it "the ripe fruits" of the Republican groups. Cries
of "treason" and clamor for military action to put down

the whiskeymen rose from the Federalists. Washington ordered the rebels to return to their homes and called up 13,000 state militia. When negotiations failed, he himself rode at the head of troops toward the embattled region. It was one of the first demonstrations of the power of the federal government. The threat of force and pleas from Pennsylvania politicians persuaded the farmers to go home before the troops reached them. Two farmers were arrested, tried for treason, convicted, sentenced to death—and then pardoned.

The stiff taxation of the farmers was unjust. But in addition the treatment of frontier resistance as a treasonable uprising against the government was a threat to civil liberties. Hamilton seized on the Whiskey Rebellion to weaken constitutional rights and intimidate the Republicans. Unfortunately he was able to make use of Washington in doing it. The whiskey rebels were wrong to protest an injustice by armed resistance. It was not the right way to correct a wrong. But there was something wrong, too, with gentlemen in power; they showed they had no notion of the problems troubling poor farmers.

Turning to foreign affairs, Washington had to make a grave political decision when Louis XVI was beheaded, and France declared herself a republic. Should the United States recognize the new French revolutionary regime? That would anger the other European powers and the Federalists at home. But not to recognize would anger the French people and the American Republicans. Washington decided for recognition. He believed every nation had the right to determine its own form of government, just as the Americans had when they broke from Britain.

But when France and Britain started fighting, it created a great issue between the Americans who took one side or the other of the rival powers. France had been our ally since the treaty of 1778. She had sent men and money to help us win independence from Britain. We had signed a treaty of mutual aid with her. Should we still be bound by that treaty? Hamilton argued that the treaty died when Louis XVI died. Jefferson replied that the treaty was still in force, for we were allied to the French nation, not to a monarch.

Both men agreed with the president that national self-interest, not political enthusiasms, should be the government's guide. To back either side in this war might be fatal to young America. It was better to avoid involvement, at almost any cost. In April 1793, the president issued a Proclamation of Neutrality. The United States, it said, would keep out of the war in Europe.

The war between Great Britain and France intensified the bad feeling between Federalists and Democratic-Republicans. In spite of the neutrality Washington had declared, the country barely escaped war with Britain. The British began to seize American cargoes headed for French ports, and to take sailors off American ships and force them to serve in the Royal Navy. The British multiplied trouble by encouraging the Indians in the Northwest to make war on the Americans. Some Democratic-Republicans called for war against Britain.

But the president would have no war. In May 1794 he sent Chief Justice John Jay to London to negotiate a treaty. His was a brutally hard task, made worse by the split over foreign policy at home and the attempts of many to interfere with his mission behind his back. After a year's troubled labor Jay brought back a treaty which he knew made too many concessions to Britain but which might prevent a disastrous war. The text was leaked to a Jeffersonian editor before Washington was ready to make it public. It evoked howls of outrage from the opposition and charges that someone had been bought off with British gold.

Washington had a difficult decision to make. If he refused the treaty, war with England was almost certain. If he accepted it, with all its weaknesses, then the interparty conflict would be painfully magnified. A realist, he decided that acceptance of the terms was the only way to preserve peace. He sent the treaty to the Senate where it was barely approved by the necessary two-thirds vote.

As the year 1795 ended, Washington had managed skillfully to avoid war and to make the country more secure than ever before in its brief history. He had steered the best course he could between Europe's rivalries, and without using military force had turned them to America's advantage.

The same year saw a complete change in Washington's cabinet. Jefferson had resigned at the end of 1793. Now Hamilton and others quit too, and in making new appointments the president chose only Federalists. The loss of Jefferson was a bad setback for Washington. No longer did he have the man close at hand to help balance the Federalist with the Republican point of view. And Jefferson out of office was the more free to lead the opposition. As he left Philadelphia, Jefferson remarked on the drop in Washington's energy, the dulling of his appetite for work, the increase in his desire for rest and quiet, and the "willingness to let others act or even think for him."

Yet Washington still seemed an impressive statesman to visitors. An Englishman meeting him in the spring of 1796 said that the president looked like "the great and good man he really was"—calm, dignified, erect. Inwardly, however, Washington felt he could not leave office soon enough. He had no desire to run for the presidency a third time, although it was clear he would easily be reelected. He no longer believed he was badly needed to hold the nation together. The Republican press hurt him when it charged him with faults he did not have and invented mistakes he had not made. Of course there had been blunders in his administration, but he had never been guilty of "a *willful* error," he said.

He began to think about preparing a Farewell Address, to let the country know he would retire to his beloved Mount Vernon at the end of this second term. He started with the few pages Madison had drafted for him back in 1792 when he had thought of leaving office at the end of his first term. He added new thoughts to it and asked Hamilton to rework it. He wanted no changes in his ideas, only to have them appear "in a plain style and be handed to the public in an honest, unaffected, simple garb." Hamilton wrote out two versions for the president's consideration, then the two men sat down together to put the Farewell in final form.

Washington did not deliver the famous address as a speech to an audience. Instead, he handed it to a friendly Philadelphia newspaper, the *American Daily Advertiser*, where it was published on the second and third pages (the first page was confined to advertisements) on Sep-

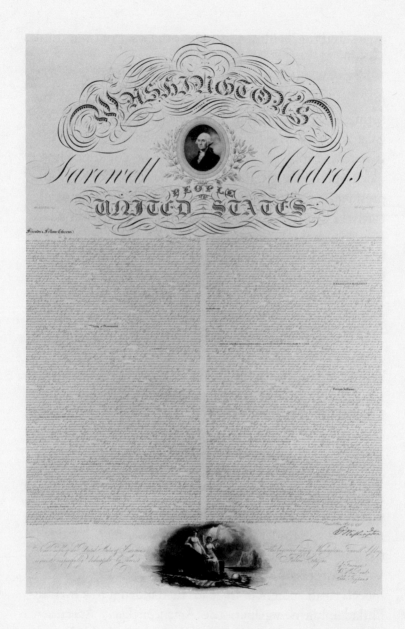

Early 19th-century engraving of
Washingtons' Farewell address

tember 19, 1796. From there the address quickly spread to newspapers throughout the country and overseas. Washington's farewell message earned an authority it has never lost. He said goodbye to his fellow Americans and advised them on the course they should follow in the future. Promote education, he said, for an enlightened public opinion is indispensable to a democracy. He asked Americans to give their loyalty to the Union, to reject any attempts to separate one part from the rest or to weaken the sacred ties that now bound them together. He hoped they would maintain a strong central government but without limiting liberty. He attacked partisan passions that would foster division or foreign intrigues or encourage the rule of minorities or demagogues. He wanted Americans to live in peace and harmony with all nations, and to stay clear of foreign entanglements and practice a true neutrality. Ending on a personal note, he hoped the country would view his defects and mistakes understandingly, remembering the many years of his life he had devoted to its service.

With his last term coming to a close, he made arrangements for moving back to Mount Vernon. On February 22, 1797, there was a fine celebration of his last birthday while in office, with Republicans joining Federalists in a farewell spirit. On March 4, Washington put on a black suit and a military hat, hung a long blue coat on his shoulders, and walked alone to the chamber of the House of Representatives to attend the inaugural ceremony for the new president, John Adams, and the new vice-president, Thomas Jefferson. As he came through the door a great ovation greeted the retiring president. He sat beside Jefferson while Adams took the oath of office. People wept to see their hero leaving public life forever. He waited for Adams and Jefferson to depart, then walked home, a crowd following him. In the evening there was a splendid farewell dinner. On March 8 he went to say goodbye to President Adams, and the next morning started home with Martha.

CHAPTER THIRTEEN

Let Me Go Quietly

*F*or the last time Washington retreated to what he called "the shades of my own Vine and Fig tree." He loved life at Mount Vernon. There was plenty for him to do: the fields and buildings badly needed care. For a time he and Martha lived in a litter of dirt made by masons, painters, and carpenters repairing the mansion and the outbuildings. From Philadelphia by sea came a sloop with his cargo of household goods—furniture plus 97 boxes, 14 trunks, 43 casks, 13 packages, 3 hampers—to be moved into Mount Vernon. With it came his beloved aide, Toby Lear, carrying news of what John Adams was doing.

Again Washington found his business affairs in poor shape. Income from his crops and rents was painfully low. His salary as President had ended, and there was no pension to replace it. (Not until the 1900s would Congress provide retirement funds for the chief of state.) Debts owed him were paid only in dribbles, and his taxes were heavy. He tried to make ends meet by selling off some land holdings. He owned nearly 300 slaves, far more than the plantation could use. He could have sold those he did not need to raise cash and cut expenses, but he could not bring himself to do it. For the first time he was forced to borrow from the bank "at ruinous interest."

Personal sorrows descended upon him. He lost his sister Betty, and then his brother Charles died. George was now the last survivor of his father's second marriage. He still felt responsible for nieces, nephews, and step-grandchildren. His grandson, George Washington Parke Custis, disappointed him by dropping out of Princeton. The boy returned to live at Mount Vernon where Washington failed to get him to study on his own. When the boy flunked out of still another school, it made Washington despair of ever being able to help him become a useful citizen.

Visitors to Mount Vernon saw only the peaceful surface. The Washingtons rarely sat down to dinner by themselves. Friends came in constantly but so did strangers who said they wanted "to pay their respects" when they were really driven by curiosity to see the most admired American. Instead of enjoying a private life, Washington felt more like a tavern-keeper. The life wearied the aging Martha to sickness, which distressed him sorely.

In his diary he noted the change of seasons, the turns in the weather, the visitors, the death of old friends, the birth of a daughter to a niece. The loneliness of old age saddened him. He wrote a long letter to England, to Sally Fairfax, the woman he had loved in youth. She was a widow now, and he had not heard from her in twenty-five years. He told her how much she had meant to him, and urged her to return to her old home in Virginia. But if she replied, there is no record of it.

Mount Vernon

Suddenly the country called him again to service.
Relations between France and the United States had got
so bad that war seemed certain to break out. And America had nothing but a small band of regulars for an army.
President Adams insisted Washington raise an army and
take command of it. Sixty-six years old now, hating to

return to public life, expecting death before long, he nevertheless could not refuse the duty. Just as he received his commission as Lieutenant General he came down with a serious fever and lost twenty pounds. Nevertheless he began to organize the new army while advising Adams to negotiate a fair settlement with France. No war came, and the patriot was able to turn planter again.

But he could not cut himself clear of politics. Entering office, he had been almost a demigod above personal attack. Still, the Republican press in his second term had not let him alone. While president, though he had not publicly lined up with the Federalists, he was thought to be more on their side than Jefferson's. Out of office, his prestige was borrowed by the Federalists whenever they needed it. In the anti-French hysteria that erupted over the prospect of war with that nation, Congress had adopted the Alien and Sedition Acts. The Alien Act let the president expel any foreigner (presumably French) he considered dangerous. The Sedition Act was aimed at publishers, editors, writers, and anyone else who dared opposed Adams's Federalist policies. It called for punishing anyone guilty of printing or writing or uttering false and malicious words intended to defame the government or arouse public hatred against it. Washington had always believed the United States should be a haven for those oppressed abroad. Even when newspapers had slandered him, he had defended freedom of the press. Now, however, in his last days, he supported Adams when the president signed the bad bills.

The Alien and Sedition Acts led to the jailing of Republican editors and even a Congressman who continued to criticize Federalist leaders and their policies.

The Republicans attacked the laws as unnecessary, despotic, and unconstitutional. It is a pity that Washington forgot his own words, spoken only shortly before: "To expect that all men should think alike upon political, more than on religious or other subjects, would be to look for a change in the order of nature."

In February 1799 the nation celebrated Washington's 67th birthday. This year it was especially joyous at Mount Vernon because of the candlelight wedding of two young relatives, Lawrence Lewis and Nelly Custis. In his letters and conversations Washington more and more often spoke of the limited time left to him. Not that he feared death; he simply wanted to leave his affairs in good order. What his ambition, energy, and luck had brought him in worldly goods he meant to distribute with great care. On July 9 he wrote out his will. He left to his "dearly beloved wife" Martha the use and benefit of his whole estate for the term of her life, with other bequests to family and friends. In his will he arranged for the freedom of all his slaves after Martha's death. (He was the only one of the Virginia founding fathers to do this.) His executors were instructed to provide for the aged slaves, and to see that the young ones were supported until maturity and taught to read and write. He set aside some funds to finance schools and found a national university, a dream of his never to be realized.

Washington was in good health that summer and fall, but Martha was ill for several weeks. On a mean December morning, he went for his usual ride over the plantation. Snow, sleet, and then rain soaked through his greatcoat, but it did not make him cut short the five-hour ride. At night, snow fell again, whitening the fields.

Portraits of George and Martha Washington painted
by John Trumbull in 1795. They once hung in
the Washingtons' bedroom at Mount Vernon.

The next morning his throat was sore, and he thought
it best to stay indoors. An hour before sunset the weather
cleared, and he went out to the front lawn to mark trees
he wanted cut down. That evening his voice was hoarse;
still, he read aloud to Martha as he often did.

He went to bed in good spirits, refusing to take
anything for what he thought was a trivial, passing cold.
Hours before dawn on December 14th he woke with an
acute fever. Martha wanted to send for help but he wouldn't
let her get up in the wintry cold. At sunrise he could
barely breathe or speak. Lear sent for Washington's lifetime friend, Dr. James Craik. While waiting for him to
arrive, the clerk Rawlins began to bleed Washington.

Seeing the man tremble, Washington said, "Don't
be afraid." Martha thought the copious flow of blood too

much and signalled to stop, but Washington managed to shake his head and say, "More." There was no change after the procedure was stopped. At eight he wished to be helped into his clothes and to a chair by the fire where he sat silently for two hours. Dr. Craik arrived and bled him. Nothing given him could relieve his throat; he felt he was suffocating. Two other physicians Dr. Craik had sent for hurried in to examine him. Near noon, a third bleeding. Still no change. A fourth bleeding. Again no change for the better. Struggling to breathe, Washington tried to shift position in bed in the hope of relieving his pain. Lear lay down beside him to raise the feeble body and tenderly turn it. In the late afternoon Washington motioned Martha to his bedside, and asked her to get his will from his desk and put it in her closet.

Lear moved to Washington's side and took his hand. "I find I am going," Washington said; "my breath cannot continue long." He asked to be placed in his chair again, sat there half an hour, then was taken back to his bed. Lear helped him sit up against the pillows and Washington said in a low voice, "I feel myself going. I thank you for your attention. You had better not take any more trouble about me, but let me go off quietly. I cannot last long."

Then Lear lowered him gently. Toward ten that night Lear saw he was trying to speak, and leaned close to hear him say, "I am just going." He asked that he not be buried until two days had gone by; he was afraid he might wake up in the coffin. Martha watched from the foot of the bed. A few minutes later his breathing eased, and he died. "Is he gone?" Martha asked as Dr. Craik gently closed Washington's eyes. " 'Tis well," she said.

"All is over now. I have no more trials to pass through. I shall soon follow him."

He was buried in the family vault in Mount Vernon. Less than eighteen months later, Martha died.

"His integrity was most pure," Jefferson said, "his justice the most inflexible."

FURTHER READING

Readers who want to know more about George Washington will find library shelves loaded with books about his life and times. His papers are located principally in the Library of Congress. The editors of the *George Washington Papers* have already collected 135,000 documents pertaining to Washington and so far have issued 11 of the 70 to 80 volumes they expect to publish through the University Press of Virginia. The same press has published Washington's *Diaries* in six volumes, and four volumes of his correspondence. A one-volume selection of his letters, edited by Thomas J. Fleming, is called *Affectionately Yours, George Washington* (Norton, 1968). It offers a self-portrait in letters to his friends.

Hundreds of biographies of Washington have appeared, some mythmaking (the cherry tree chopped down and the dollar flung across the Potomac), some debunking (the man was really a coward or a liar or whatever would make him look bad), and others serious and honest, though of course shaped by whatever bias the writer has. These lives began coming out within a few years of Washington's death. You can always expect to see still another this year or next. Every generation feels the need to reinterpret the man according to its own lights.

Among the most important modern lives are Douglas S. Freeman's enormously detailed and invaluable study, *George Washington: A Biography*, seven volumes (Scribner's, 1948-57). Richard Harwell abridged Freeman's work for the one-volume paperback, *George Washington* (Scribner's, 1985). Later, James Thomas Flexner produced a massive four-volume life, *George Washington*, (Little Brown, 1965–72). Then Flexner rewrote his biography for the one-volume paperback, *Washington: The Indispensable Man*, (Signet, 1984). Another good paperback life is *George Washington: Man and Monument*, by the English historian, Marcus Cunliffe, (Mentor, 1982).

Many authors have approached Washington's life from some special angle. There are books about his ancestry, his estate, his youth, as the country gentleman, as the commanding general in the Revolution, as presiding officer of the Constitutional Convention, about his two terms in the presidency, even about his expense account. Worth looking for too are collections of critical essays on Washington or comments on him by his contemporaries.

As for the setting of his life, the eighteenth century, there are scores of studies to illuminate its diverse aspects. You will find books about his Virginia and the other colonies, about views of slavery and race in that time, about the Indians and the wars involving them, about the colonial frontier, trade and commerce, agricultural life, and on and on.

The American Revolution itself, what led up to it and its consequences, are treated in many narrative and analytical works. There are military, political, social histories of the Revolution, as well as collections of fascinating diaries and letters of men who fought the battles, and accounts of both the Patriots and the Loyalists, or Tories. How the British viewed the struggle is another significant facet to explore.

The creation of our national government and its development are discussed in many books. These cover such topics as the Articles of Confederation, the Continental Congress, the rise of political parties, the role of the northern and southern regions, and the Constitutional Convention.

The shaping of the presidency during Washington's terms, the differences between Federalists and Republicans, the handling of domestic affairs and international relations, are the subjects of several studies. Finally the lives of many people Washington knew and worked with, who became friends or enemies, can be read to cast light on Washington and his relationships. Here I refer to such figures as Thomas Jefferson, Alexander Hamilton, John Adams, James Madison, Benedict Arnold, Marquis de Lafayette, and many of the other leading officers of the Revolution, both American and foreign.

INDEX

Adams, John, 111, 141, 144, 167, 171
Adams, Samuel, 70, 74
Alien and Sedition Acts, 172–73
Allen, Ethan, 78
American Revolution
  Blacks in, 117–18
  causes of, 67–79
  lessons learned from, 116
  see also Washington, George; *and names of battle sites*
Arnold, Benedict, 87, 106
André, Major John, 106
Articles of Confederation, 100, 125

Belvoir, 21–22, 29
Bennington, 96
Bill of Rights, 138, 139, 147–48
Boston Massacre, 71
Boston siege, 88, 103
Boston Tea Party, 74
Braddock, General Edward, 43
Brandywine River, 97
Breed's Hill, 87
Britain, wars with France, 33–53, 67, 163
British America, 15–17
Bunker Hill, 87
Burgoyne, General John, 95, 96, 98

Camden, 104

Henry, Patrick, 70, 76, 117
Hessians, 92
Holland, 98
Houdon, Jean Antoine, 121
Howe, General William, 92, 93, 96, 97

Immigrants, 15–16
Indentured servants, 15, 25
Independence, American, 111
Indians, 27–28, 34, 36, 37, 41–42, 44, 48, 49–50, 67, 68, 95, 155–56, 163

Jacobins, 158–59
Jay, John, 111, 139, 145, 148, 163–64
Jefferson, Thomas, 89, 115, 116, 123, 145, 148–53, 156, 157, 160, 164, 167, 176
Jones, Captain John Paul, 98, 106

King's Mountain, 105
Knox, General Henry, 145

Lafayette, Marquis de, 98–100, 103, 115, 118, 139
Lear, Tobias, 123, 124, 144, 169, 174–75
Lee, General Charles, 103
Lee, Richard Henry, 89
Lee, William, 117–18
L'Enfant, Pierre, 157
Lewis, Lawrence, 173
Lexington, 89
Livingston, Robert, 143
Long Island, 92
Louis XV, King, 36
Louis XVI, King, 98, 162, 163
Loyalists.
   See Tories

Madison, James, 129, 135, 139, 153
Mercer, George, 55
Monmouth, 103
Morris, Robert, 158
Morristown, 105
Mount Vernon, 17, 26, 31, 43, 49, 56–61, 103, 111, 115–27, 138, 141, 154, 157, 158, 165, 167, 169–76
Mutinies, 105

ABOUT THE AUTHOR

Milton Meltzer has written over sixty books in the fields of biography, history, and social reform. Many of his books have received awards, most recently for *Ain't Gonna Study War No More*. His *George Washington* is the latest of fifteen biographies. Among his subjects are Mark Twain, Langston Hughes, Betty Friedan, Dorothea Lange, Winnie Mandela and Thoreau. His series on American minorities includes *The Black Americans*, *The Chinese Americans*, *The Hispanic Americans*, and *The Jewish Americans*. In his work he has treated many social issues including poverty, terrorism, the Ku Klux Klan, human rights, and slavery.

Mr. Meltzer was born in Worcester, Massachusetts, and educated at Columbia University. He lives with his wife in New York City. They have two daughters, Jane and Amy.